THE

Loneliness
COMPANION

THE
Loneliness
COMPANION

—

A PRACTICAL GUIDE FOR IMPROVING YOUR SELF-ESTEEM AND FINDING COMFORT IN YOURSELF

SHREIN H. BAHRAMI

ROCKRIDGE
PRESS

For general information on our other products and services or to obtain technical support, please contact our Customer Care Department within the United States at (866) 744-2665, or outside the United States at (510) 253-0500.

Rockridge Press publishes its books in a variety of electronic and print formats. Some content that appears in print may not be available in electronic books, and vice versa.

Interior and Cover Designer: Lindsey Dekker
Art Producer: Michael Hardgrove
Editor: Emily Angell
Production Editor: Jose Olivera
Author photo courtesy of © Tory Putnam

ISBN: Print 978-1-64152-702-6 eBook 978-1-64152-703-3

R0

I DEDICATE THIS BOOK
TO MY SISTERS,
RAQUEL, ROYA, NASREIN, AND
MINA, MY GREATEST BALMS
TO LONELINESS.

CONTENTS

INTRODUCTION

◆ ◆ ◆

*A*s I began to tell family, friends, and colleagues my plan to write a book on loneliness, time and again I was surprised by their responses. Instead of discomfort or deflection, they showed genuine interest in the topic, often opening up about their own experiences. Even strangers I chatted with as I sat writing in coffee shops remarked how important they felt this issue is and pondered why people seem more isolated from each other than ever before. Many pointed to the shift our society has made from one once focused on community and family to one that prizes independence and individualism. Consequently, relationships feel more fleeting and superficial as work and external markers of success take precedent. Others wondered about the impact of social media and whether or not it has actually improved our ability to connect. These questions and observations inspired me to continue my research and understanding of our relationship with loneliness and how to heal it.

As a psychotherapist, I have the unique opportunity of being invited into my clients' personal journeys as they seek to heal the parts of themselves that are in pain and yearn for something different. Often, the most challenging work has been in making changes in their relationships, whether it be with family, friends, colleagues, or intimate partners.

When faced with so many elements out of our control because another person's needs, wants, and opinions are involved, we understandably want to give up or surrender to the status quo. Yet the key to change rests within you and your ability to choose your perspective. Particularly in intimate relationships, whether you are recovering after a breakup, surviving the highs and lows of dating, or weathering the storms of a long-term relationship, the way in which you navigate your experiences significantly impacts your level of loneliness. Each person's life is unique, yet many of our challenges are universal. We often suffer silently, believing we are the only ones going through it. The lens through which we view our lives and judge our current experiences is largely influenced by the past, making it difficult to see things in a different way and get unstuck from patterns that no longer serve us.

After a decade of clinical work and training, my approach is composed of techniques from several evidence-based treatment models that address the mind, body, and spirit, resulting in lasting change. In my sessions with clients, I support them in applying these tools to their own challenges and have witnessed powerful, life-changing outcomes.

My hope is that you find this book to be a comprehensive, yet approachable guide to addressing your loneliness and improving your sense of connection with others. Each chapter will explore a facet of loneliness, from the causes and impact on your health to how you can lessen its grip on your life and enjoy moments of solitude. I have included multiple exercises within each chapter to help you practice and apply the tools to your life right now. I recommend using a journal while you make your way through this book, as there will be writing prompts for reflection on your own experiences. Lastly, peppered throughout each chapter are stories of my own clients' journeys while addressing their challenges with connection. My intention for including these stories is to help you feel less alone as you make this journey and to be a source of hope that change is possible.

I am so glad you have chosen to take this step in addressing your loneliness. I understand how difficult it may have been just to acknowledge a desire to make a change in this area of your life. Yet nearly every important change we make in our lives begins with resistance. I am certain that if you continue reading and push through the internal barriers, you will come away with a greater understanding of why your struggle with loneliness exists, why it isn't your fault, and how to go about creating the types of relationships you desire as you move forward.

We're born alone, live alone, and die alone. Only through love and friendship can we create the illusion for the moment that we're not alone.
—ORSON WELLES

The most terrible poverty is loneliness and the feeling of being unloved.
—MOTHER TERESA

CHAPTER 1

What We Mean When We Talk About Loneliness

Loneliness may be one of the most difficult feelings to experience. It is uncomfortable to talk about and no one wants to admit they are lonely. Yet we all feel it. Loneliness does not discriminate by race, age, or socioeconomic status. Whether you struggle with fleeting moments of loneliness or feel it as a daily presence, understanding that you are not the only one who feels this way is essential to healing. Gaining more knowledge of the underlying causes of loneliness will help you let go of false beliefs and empower you to take further steps toward positive change. This chapter will provide an overview of the most current research and statistics on loneliness and the impact it has on relationships, productivity, and overall health. You may find the results of these studies alarming, but they are meant to provide perspective, to reveal the common humanity of the loneliness experience, and to illustrate how worthwhile it is to invest your time improving your connections with others.

WHAT IS LONELINESS?

Like most feelings, loneliness is a difficult emotion to define. Every person has their own interpretation of what it feels like to be lonely and that perspective is founded on the sum of their individual experiences. However, loneliness impacts each and every one of us in some form. If you are not experiencing it right now, someone close to you is. Learning about its far-reaching effects is integral to both understanding and changing your unique experience with loneliness. In 2018, Cigna, a global health service company, conducted a survey of 20,000 Americans to examine the prevalence of loneliness in people's lives. The survey revealed that loneliness is an epidemic in our country. According to the findings, about one in six adults has a clinical mental health condition and the one common factor across the varied mental health diagnoses is loneliness. The study also revealed that loneliness is correlated with increased use of sick leave, and it has the same impact on a person's health as smoking the equivalent of 15 cigarettes a day.

On a daily basis, many people experience feeling lonely to some degree. It is an unfortunate irony that such a common feeling is accompanied by social stigma and shame. We don't want to admit that we are lonely, and we certainly don't want to ask for help There are a host of myths surrounding loneliness that contribute to our secretiveness about it. For example, believing that a person who has many friends and goes out every weekend can't possibly be lonely. Yet even when surrounded by people, that individual may feel utterly alone. Another myth is the presumption that, if a person is single, they must be perpetually lonely. While this may be true for some, not all who are alone are lonely. One person can feel lonely while another can be perfectly at peace being alone.

One key difference between loneliness and aloneness, or loneliness and solitude, is the element of choice. We choose when we want to leave a party or take a vacation alone, but experiencing loneliness is not a matter of choice. Another distinction is the perspective one adopts. Given the same situation, each of us will have different ways of relating and assigning meaning. Like experiencing disappointment or anxiety, the feeling of loneliness is unique to each of us because of our beliefs, thoughts, and past experiences. For example, the person who felt lonely at the party may have been physically surrounded by several friendly people eager to engage in conversation, yet may have felt alienated and lacked a sense of genuine connection. Even though it seems contradictory, being in a group of people (especially during the holidays) is a common trigger for feeling insecure or unaccepting of ourselves. Regardless of your closeness to others, no one will ever truly know what it is like to be you or feel exactly the same way. Yet we long to belong. As social creatures who seek approval and connection (almost as much as air, water, and shelter), we must find a way to balance this duality. To be lonely, therefore, is to suffer because of an unmet need for authentic social connection.

Loneliness is a very normal, and in fact healthy, human experience. It has meaning and purpose just like any other emotion—it provides a cue and a clue to an unmet need. Unfortunately, because of the stigma that surrounds loneliness, the emotional experience can become unnecessarily exacerbated, contributing to even greater suffering. The painful impact of loneliness would undoubtedly diminish if it were an emotion that was more openly shared and socially accepted. In spite of how taboo it may feel to talk about loneliness, remind yourself how many people are struggling with it. Many people, including you perhaps, are quite good at hiding their loneliness. Unfortunately, these masks of inauthenticity reinforce the disconnection, isolation, and fear of judgment. It is impossible to ever bring an end to feeling lonely. Thus, the goal is not to eradicate the feeling completely, but instead find ways to manage it and diminish its influence on your life.

THE COMMON DENOMINATORS OF HAPPINESS

In Dan Buettner's book *The Blue Zones of Happiness*, he posits that in order to be happy, you should ideally have at least three friends who you can count on and with whom you can have meaningful conversations. Further, he found that after surveying two million people in the workforce worldwide, the most important determinant of a person's happiness at their job was having a best friend at work. This, and other studies like it, validate the importance of the *quality* of relationships with coworkers as a strong predictor of the degree of loneliness experienced by an individual. Those who rated their coworker relationships as good, very good, or excellent were significantly more likely to be in good to excellent overall health. Ultimately, Buettner's research found that our lifestyle is key to living a satisfying life, and the most important factors that contribute to health and longevity include not only the way we eat and move, but the quality of our engagement with others.

COMMON CAUSES OF LONELINESS

Despite wonderful advances in modern technology and health care, as a Western society, we still have work to do on the social and emotional front. As a culture, we place great value on individualism, which conflicts with the intrinsic need of humans to be part of a community. Individualistic societies predicate success on competition ("you versus me"), as opposed to collectivistic societies, which define success by collaboration ("you with me"). Thus, societal structures play a role in the experience of loneliness. This is well described by Joseph Hartog who, in *The Anatomy of Loneliness*, states, "In a society that seeks to cultivate autonomous individuals who have great mobility and tenuous attachments, loneliness will be commonplace." Finding a balance between competing to get ahead and collaborating for the good of the group has become exceedingly challenging within an individualistic society.

For example, according to a 2019 CNN report, the pressure to get into top schools is more intense than ever. Adolescents are expected to choose a major that will ideally relate to their lifelong career path and then excel in it at any cost until they have reached the highest rung of the professional ladder. Taking time between high school and college to volunteer, explore different careers, or travel is often sidelined for fear of missing out and falling behind. No wonder loneliness is an epidemic; it is a natural by-product of such stoic and competitive individualism.

Another common cause of loneliness is our lack of education on how to identify and express our emotions. Even the most sensitive, compassionate, and well-intentioned individual may have difficulty communicating their wants and needs to a partner. No two people will ever have the exact same emotional response to a shared experience. We are all different, due to a unique blend of nature (inborn temperament) and nurture (the environment in which we were raised). Our temperament, and the temperaments of our caregivers, typically correlate to our views about being alone. The closeness demonstrated between parent partners acts as a "teaching model" for their children. As children observe their parents relating to one another, in overt and covert ways, they determine what is acceptable emotional expression and adjust their behavior to fit the family relational style. Depending on the level of emotional support available, children learn how to seek acceptance and receive praise, which contributes to their sense of worth and value as an individual. For many families, the emotional support was minimal or conditional—often due to "faulty learning models" that have been handed down through the generations.

Emotional learning models within our childhood families, and the specific role we may have occupied in our particular family system, often carry over to the relationships we create with friends, colleagues, and romantic partners. If you were the caretaker in the family, you may unwittingly re-create relationships in which you overly concern yourself with others' feelings or needs. This behavior may elicit a familiar sense of connection in the beginning of a new relationship, but often leads to burnout, resentment, and the fear that your only value to the other person comes from what you do for them. It can lead to a reenactment of old family lessons; if you don't perform these services and provide limitless emotional support, the other person will revoke their love and acceptance.

Perhaps you felt alienated in your family of origin because of your interests, appearance, or temperament, so you have grown to be hypervigilant, always scouting for potential differences between you and others. You may try to overcorrect or hide parts of yourself to manage your fear of being judged as inadequate and therefore unlikable. Alternatively, you may have been overvalued for one aspect of yourself, resulting in feeling disconnected because you are not expressing all facets of yourself. Often, things like our relationship status, appearance, education, and level of wealth are parts of ourselves that we critique harshly, believing others are viewing them just as negatively. As a result, we erect emotional walls for protection, which further isolates us and reinforces our negative self-assessment, exacerbating our feelings of loneliness.

Common causes of loneliness include:
- Growing up in a culture that values individualism over community/group
- A lack of education on how to identify and express our emotions
- "Emotional learning models" from our childhood family that influence our actions as an adult

SELF-REFLECTION

Let's pause for a moment and check in on your thoughts regarding the information provided so far and your intentions for reading this book. Writing self-reflection responses in a journal is an effective way to process your experience. It provides you with an opportunity to look back at your previously assembled thoughts after you finish reading the entire book, and to see what (if any) of your perspectives may have changed.

Some things to consider when reflecting and assembling your journal writings for this chapter could include:

- Were you surprised to learn that loneliness is quite common? What about the prevalence of loneliness was most surprising or reassuring to you?
- What brought you to this book? Have you considered reading a book on this topic for some time? If so, what kept you from taking this step previously?
- What are you hoping will change in your life after reading this book? Be as specific and clear as you can. For example, instead of "I want to stop feeling lonely," you could write about your desire to improve your relationship with a sibling you've lost touch with, or develop a greater sense of belonging with your friends.

COMMON SYMPTOMS
OF LONELINESS

The emotional and physical sensations of loneliness present themselves in a variety of ways.
Loneliness is not an emotion that is commonly
visible, as emotions such as happiness and anger
can be. Some people are surprised when they
realize what they are feeling is loneliness and
turn to numbing behaviors in order to remain in
denial. As with the sensations that accompany
hunger, the physical manifestations of loneliness
are also a sign of a yearning for something.
When we are hungry, we may get cranky, commonly referred to as "hangry," and feel unable to
focus or expend any physical energy. After we
eat and are satisfied, the discomfort of hunger
ceases and we arrive at a sense of physical
contentment. Thus, we don't have to be pre-
occupied with food anymore and can move on
to other things. Similarly, if we do not feel met
in our relationships, we will yearn relationally
for something more. The physical symptoms of
loneliness is our bodies' way of communicating
the lack of connection and a signal to get us to
attend to it. If regularly ignored, our thoughts
become distorted and fear-based, such as "no
one will ever really understand me," or "I will

never be enough, so I should withdraw or distance myself from this other person." Ultimately, this leads to an endless loop of suffering: need, pain, denial, protective yet harmful behavior, isolation, unmet need, pain, denial, and so on. To the contrary, when we feel good in our social relationships, our need for connection is satisfied. We are then able to focus on other areas of our life, knowing that our desire for authentic connection can be met whenever the need arises again (which it naturally will).

Psychological Symptoms

To conserve mental energy and avoid potential danger, our minds create decision-making shortcuts. When we are lonely, these cognitive shortcuts typically lead to distorted perceptions, viewing social interactions through a guarded and suspicious lens. For example, when meeting someone new for a first date, you may be on high alert for any negative judgment related to something about yourself you believe to be deficient (job, relationship status, level of education, appearance, etc.). Consequently, you may regard a natural pause in conversation as evidence that the other person has discovered, and is disappointed by, your personal shortcomings (the cognitive shortcut). You then begin to gather further "evidence" that the other person is uninterested in you or you may try to over-compensate for your self-perceived flaws. Any positive evidence to the contrary, like a smile or compliment, may go unnoticed or discounted as a courtesy or a sign of pity.

Cognitive shortcuts become entrenched over time and interfere with our ability to make fair and objective relational evaluations, thus rendering us incapable of responding accurately to our social experiences. These processes also disrupt the connection of our internal percep-tions to external reality. Sometimes the distorted shortcuts morph into more detrimental mental health conditions, like social anxiety, paranoia, or phobias. For example, a friend recently shared a disastrous, brief first date in which, after asking her date what he did for work, he angrily remarked how annoyed he was with that question and refused to answer. Surprised by his response, she explained that she didn't mean to offend and could relate to feeling frustrated with work and her intention was just to get to know him. Yet he became even more defensive, remarking how rude a question it was and that it was an asinine way of getting to know someone.

She felt like he had put up a wall and ended the date quickly thereafter.

Even when we are conscious of the negative impact of taking a cognitive shortcut, and wholeheartedly want to make a change, our minds continue to prefer the shortcuts in order to find quick, albeit temporary, fixes. These may include deciding to change something external, such as updating a wardrobe, losing weight, or working harder for a promotion. When, ultimately, those changes do not work or do not work long-term in helping us feel accepted, liked, and connected (and they won't, since the cognitive distortions persist and continue to skew one's perspective and engagement), the disappointment that follows ultimately triggers a downward spiral of helplessness and hopeless-ness. Turning to alcohol or a night of bingeing on food and Netflix is an understandable alternative when it feels like the efforts you are making to be seen and belong are never enough.

Psychological symptoms of loneliness include:

- Ruminating thoughts
- Irritability or short temper
- Inability to focus
- Paranoia
- Catastrophizing, thinking the worst
- Constant fight or flight mode
- Depressed mood
- Lack of interest in being outdoors
- Lack of interest in exercise

Physical Symptoms

The physical signs of loneliness are varied and manifest in ways that are detrimental to our health. Biologically, when we are lonely, our bodies produce greater amounts of the stress hormone epinephrine, more commonly known as adrenaline. Adrenaline triggers an increase in heart rate, blood pressure, and sugar metabolism.

Loneliness also has a detrimental effect on the brain's ability to rest and restore itself. Sleep quality is just as important to our overall health as diet and exercise. Research has shown that individuals who receive quality sleep, and who sleep what they perceive to be the right amount of time, show the lowest loneliness score indicators, versus those who do not receive quality sleep or who sleep less.

When we are feeling isolated and lonely, decisions made in the moment to alleviate pain tend not to be the most beneficial for our health. For example, alcohol and controlled substances have more or less become culturally acceptable lubricants for social anxiety. But in excess they can lead to misuse, addiction, and even greater health issues. It became very clear in my work with my client Ryan that his relationship with alcohol was a trigger and numbing agent for his loneliness. Since starting a full-time job after college, his routine had largely remained the same: working late during the week and spending his evenings alone in his apartment. Ryan would then pack his weekend full of socializing with friends, which almost always involved alcohol. Over the last few years, Ryan felt more self-conscious around his friends as they had all entered serious relationships while he remained single. He began canceling plans at the last minute and staying in his apartment more and more, sometimes going the whole weekend without leaving. His alcohol consumption increased and became a daily occurrence, averaging a bottle of wine each night. Ryan was tired of how terrible his body felt in the morning after a night of drinking, yet feared it would be impossible to get through a night alone without it.

Physical symptoms of loneliness include:
- Racing heart
- Tearfulness
- Tangential speaking
- Weight gain
- Feeling sick—upset stomach, headache

Mind-Body Connection

Understanding the connection between your mind and body will be instrumental in addressing your loneliness. Making this connection can feel uncomfortable, yet it is a significant factor in how you decide to react and respond in certain situations. For instance, if I ask you to imagine giving a talk to a group of 500 people tomorrow, what reaction does that elicit in your body? I am sorry to do that to you, but your physiological response is evidence of the mind-body connection as well as your body's instantaneous reaction to just the thought of a potentially unnerving experience, regardless of whether the perceived danger is real or imagined. Additionally, if you often ruminate on events that occurred in the past or what could potentially happen in the future, your body will evoke similar physiological responses needlessly, draining your mental and physical reserves. Reflecting on the past and planning for the future can be beneficial. But when our thoughts are constantly distracted from the present moment, we miss out on opportunities for connection, joy, and growth.

Mind-body symptoms of loneliness include:
- Engaging in distracting activities
- Perceived stress and struggling to cope with stress
- Numbing out
- Self-harm behaviors
- Negative body image
- Body dysmorphia
- Helplessness
- Hopelessness

MUSCLE RELAXATION MEDITATION FOR THE MIND AND BODY

Meditation is a tool that can help you reduce stress and bring you into the present moment. It can be done whenever you have a few moments to yourself and is a powerful way to reset your mind and body. I will often lead my clients through a meditation in our sessions to help them be in the present moment and connect to their inner selves. There are various forms of meditation that I will share throughout the book. This mind and body meditation will guide you to tense and release muscles in your face and upper body to facilitate an intentional connection with your muscles and a state of relaxation by releasing and letting go of tension.

- Begin the meditation by finding a comfortable seat.
- You can keep your eyes open or you may close them. It is normal that your mind will wander, and when it does, gently refocus it back on the meditation.
- Starting at the top of your head, down to the tips of your toes, become aware of any areas of tension. Doing so will help you notice the impact on your physical state.

- Inhale deeply, hold for a few seconds, and then exhale slowly.
- When you exhale, imagine slowly releasing the tension in your body.
- On your next breath, try to breathe in to the count of 8, hold for 2, and then exhale for 10.
- Again, in for 8, hold for 2, out for 10. Notice how your body feels.
- Now, squeeze your eyes shut for about 10 seconds, and then release. Take a deep breath in and out.
- Next, smile as wide as you can for 10 seconds, and then release. Feel as your face relaxes.
- Take another deep breath in and out.
- Next, lift your shoulders up to your ears and hold for 10 seconds. Then quickly drop them down.
- Breathe in and out.
- Tightly clench your fists for about 10 seconds. . . and release. Allow them to go limp.
- Pause and just breathe.
- With every exhalation, visualize slowly releasing the tension from your body.
- Inhale again . . . and slowly exhale.
- Tune in to your body being overcome with a feeling of calm and relaxation.
- Notice if there were any shifts from when you began. Pause for gratitude in taking this time to focus on your mind-body connection.

Short-Term and Long-Term Health Effects

In addition to the immediate symptoms that arise when someone experiences loneliness, there are short- and long-term health issues that can occur if loneliness becomes chronic. This information is not meant to scare you. Rather, it is meant to inform you of the realities of the effects of loneliness and equip you with knowledge and tools to improve your mental and physical health.

The connection between a person's loneliness and a person's health cannot be understated. The current generation of Americans, known as Generation Z (people born between the mid-1990s and early 2000s), has the distinction of being the loneliest generation of Americans to date. In a recent study, nearly half of participants reported sometimes or always feeling alone (46 percent) or left out (47 percent). In fact, only 53 percent reported that they had daily, meaningful social interactions. These interactions typically included such things as an in-person conversation with a friend, or quality time with a family member.

A complete definition of health encompasses not just physical well-being but emotional, psychological, and mental wellness—in other words, to accurately assess health, we must consider the mind-body connection. Even though loneliness is not a mental health disorder, it often coincides with one or more disorders, most commonly depression. The experience of each condition may involve similar thoughts and feelings, but the impact on a person's quality of life is different. Depression causes an all-encompassing lack of interest in life, a form of numbing that decreases their ability to feel concern or the ability to act. Loneliness, on the other hand, is like a fuel tank alert, signaling low levels of connection and the need to refuel. It spurs action and a desire for change. When a person struggles with both conditions, a sense of helplessness, resignation, and passivity may develop, creating even higher hurdles to clear on their path to decreasing loneliness.

In addition to depression, loneliness also coincides with high levels of stress and anxiety, particularly as a person grows older. A 2013 study conducted by Louise Hawkley and John Cacioppo called "Loneliness Matters" showed that, compared to young adults, older adults who were lonelier also reported higher quantities of objective stressors in their lives. The authors concluded that, by avoiding dealing with loneliness, over time, the protective walls a person puts up cause rifts in a variety of relationships, including with their spouse, co-workers, and community in general. Not only are the perceived stressors (for example, an issue with a neighbor) more frequent, but they are also more severe. Further, these individuals feel at a loss to change the situation, and thus are less likely to seek out emotional or practical support from others.

Importantly, the research showed that the opposite holds true for those respondents who are less lonely. This group indicated that they experience more frequent, meaningful, in-person interactions and feel overall that the status of their relationships and social skills are good. They also expressed being in good health overall and reported that their lives felt balanced. This further supports the notion that by addressing your loneliness, many areas of your life stand to improve as well.

THE NECESSITY OF SELF-CARE

There are various definitions and interpretations of what self-care is, exactly. I approach it as a discipline toward mental and physical well-being. Our culture has slowly begun to shift toward recognizing self-care as a priority and a component of a happy life. Historically, well-being took a back seat to success, relegated to something that could come once success had been achieved. In the meantime, overworking oneself to the point of exhaustion or depending on substances to make it through the day became the norm. The fear of appearing unmotivated or lazy drives us to prove ourselves at any cost. Yet living for success in the traditional sense keeps us from enjoying life right now. Life is better lived when you enjoy the journey and each day are grateful for the good that you already possess, not just for the promise of what is to come. It also requires that you prioritize the needs of your mind and body for rest, relaxation, pleasure, creativity, and joy.

THE GOOD NEWS

I understand that a great deal of this chapter may be quite sobering for you. The good news is that the most significant way to heal loneliness is within your control. Loneliness can be relieved, or at least lessened, by applying the practical advice, strategies, and exercises found in this book. The tools are evidence-based and have been proven to help anyone who is suffering from loneliness. Although this may not be the quick fix you hoped for, you have already taken a big step on this journey. Accessing help outside of ourselves, for many, can be the biggest hurdle to overcome, and having this book in your hands represents accomplishment of that feat.

THE POWER OF CONNECTION

In my therapy work with clients, I have observed time and again the impact our relationships have on our well-being. A lack of understanding and disconnection between significant others and family members is often at the heart of the therapeutic work. My clients have often expressed feeling at a loss for how to go about changing problematic dynamics with other people. In order to not rock the boat, inflict pain on the

YOUR PATH

Each chapter will include exercises to help you relate to the information in a deeper way, either through journaling, meditation, or actionable steps. Completing them as you read is ideal, but you may prefer to return to them at the conclusion of each chapter or the book. Some exercises will resonate with you and others will not. I encourage you to do what you feel comfortable with while recognizing that change only comes with action. Grab your journal and answer the following prompts:

- What is causing you to feel lonely? Try not to censor yourself. Write whatever comes to mind regarding your current experience of loneliness.
- Recall a recent time when you considered reaching out to someone but then chose not to, or when you canceled plans at the last minute. What were the reasons behind this decision? How did you feel afterward?
- What are your current forms of self-care? How much time do you currently dedicate to self-care, and are there ways you could increase it, especially as you make your way through this book?
- Take Action: Write a note to a friend you haven't spoken to in a long time. Handwritten is great, but email works, too! Let them know you are thinking of them. For example, you can start by writing, *"I haven't spoken to you in a while and I miss your_____,"* or *"The other day I thought of you when_____."*

other person, or create more conflict, they resign themselves to feeling perpetually misunderstood or estranged. Yet as they begin to take steps to face the discomfort and address the friction, as uncomfortable as it may be, the benefits of a more open and honest relationship begin to surface in ways they didn't expect.

It doesn't matter if you have 300 friends or 3, the quality of connection is much more important than the quantity. As an example, many celebrities struggle with loneliness in spite of the fact that they have scores of adoring fans. It is no wonder that many of these talented but lonely souls are the ones who eventually turn to substances, or even suicide, for relief. My hope is that with awareness, fewer people will suffer from the profound pain of isolation and disconnection.

ALONE TOGETHER

Unquestionably, the way we connect with each other has vastly changed as a result of social media. From the way we receive world news, to the way we receive updates from family members and friends, it is fair to say technology is not likely to decrease its impact on our social culture. As a rather recent phenomenon, there is not yet extensive data on the impact of technology on, or its association with, loneliness. However, a study published in January of 2019 by Brian A. Primack, MD, PhD, looked at positive and negative experiences posted or reported on social media and how such postings related to perceived social isolation. They found that if someone reported positive experiences on social media, there was no association with increased social isolation. If they reported negative experiences, it was associated with greater social isolation. These results align with the concept of negativity bias, wherein things that are seen as negative have greater effect than ones that are positive or neutral.

What if all our social media experiences were favorable? Would that be enough to satisfy our need for connection as social animals? Based on my clients' and my own experiences, I think it is important to find a balance, as with most things in life. It is equally important to ensure your needs are met virtually, as well as in person, on a regular basis. After all, there are experiences that can only come through direct personal engagement, such as sharing a warm embrace or a good laugh with a friend (versus reading "LOL" or sharing an emoticon). These moments are invaluable in deepening the connection between individuals.

CONCLUSION

In this chapter, we discussed various social and scientific perspectives pertaining to loneliness. The mental and physical symptoms of loneliness, as well as common triggers, were reviewed. You were invited to reflect on your unique journey via journaling, meditation, and actionable steps. In the next chapter, I'll provide an overview of just how influential our relationships are on the quality of our lives and how to better understand what has influenced your patterns of behavior within your relationships.

Additionally, each chapter will end with several positive affirmations related to the themes of the chapter. Reciting affirmations helps you personalize what you are reading and claim them as a possibility. As you read through them and say each one, either out loud or to yourself, notice which ones feel authentic and which ones elicit a sense of resistance. We will explore this resistance in future chapters. For the ones that resonate with you, I encourage you to write them down and place them somewhere so that you can see them daily.

SOCIAL MEDIA CHALLENGE

"A picture of a rice cake cannot satisfy hunger."
—BUDDHIST SAYING

Try not to check your social media for an entire day. Be aware of the thoughts and feelings that may be connected to the urge to log in. For example, is it a fear of missing out (FOMO), or feelings of loneliness and lack of connection? Could it be boredom or the need for a mental break? Additionally, notice if you use or consider using other forms to connect.

In your journal, write your answers to the following questions:

- Were you able to go a whole day without using any social media?
- What emotions surfaced as a result of refraining from social media?
- Were you surprised by any of the emotions that surfaced?
- As a result of experimenting with this challenge, do you intend to make any changes regarding how often you use social media?

AFFIRMATIONS

I forgive those who have harmed me
in my past and I let go of anger.

I forgive myself for perceived mistakes
I have made in the past.

I deserve to live a life I am proud of.

I am a person dedicated to living
a life of fulfillment.

I believe in the value of and engage
in regular self-care.

There are two basic motivating forces:
fear and love. When we are afraid, we
pull back from life. When we are in love,
we open to all that life has to offer with
passion, excitement, and acceptance.
We need to learn to love ourselves first, in
all our glory and our imperfections."
—JOHN LENNON

CHAPTER 2

Healing from Past Relationships

Now that you've been given an overview of the key components of relationships, we'll look more closely at how your relationships with family, friends, and romantic partners have impacted your experiences of loneliness. Relationships have the power to shape the way we feel about ourselves as well as how we relate to the world around us. Past experiences rarely remain entirely in the past, and consciously or unconsciously influence many of our choices in life. By reflecting on and learning from these experiences, we can correct faulty beliefs and problematic patterns of behavior that lead us down paths we'd prefer not to revisit. Furthermore, exploring our childhood experiences can provide tremendous insight and clarity regarding our current relational dynamics; it's like a corner piece of the puzzle of understanding why we are the way we are. One of the most prominent psychological models on relationships that we will explore is attachment theory. It illustrates why our need for connection is biological and explains why some of us have greater difficulty balancing our emotions and relating to others.

THE NECESSITY OF CONNECTION

Human beings not only crave connection, we are wired for it. For most other species, the greatest reason for being in a tribe is physical safety and survival. For humans, it is more about emotional survival. We cannot thrive in our lives unless we feel a bond with others. The positive impact of connection starts in the womb as a fetus begins to recognize familiar voices and sounds. And as soon as a baby is born, skin to skin contact with parents is strongly encouraged to foster bonding. As John Cacioppo states in his book *Loneliness: Human Nature and the Need for Human Connection*, "It takes a while for an infant to discover that she and her mother are not actually one and the same." As we grow and begin to feel the need to individuate, we do so while holding on to our need for safety through connection. This lifelong balancing act is fundamental to our experience of loneliness.

As infants, our survival depended on our caregivers. The sole way of communicating our needs to them was to cry. We cried when we were hungry, had to be changed, and wanted to be held or soothed. If these needs consistently go unmet, the infant's growth and brain development can be stunted. This phenomenon has been widely researched in studies with children in Romanian orphanages. Due to a ban on abortion and contraception by the then-communist government, the orphanages were overwhelmed and not properly staffed. Infants were left alone in their cribs for days on end. As a result of the lack of attention and nurturing, the orphans developed severe cognitive and emotional impairments. These troubling outcomes further demonstrate the biological necessity to attach.

As we move through childhood to adolescence and adulthood, our desire for connection becomes more than solely a survival mechanism. Joseph Hartog states in his book, *The Anatomy of Loneliness*, that through each stage in our life, our realization of being alone in this world becomes clearer. Some people can recall distinct moments in their childhood when they realized their parents were not all-powerful or perfect human beings. During our teen years, we learn more about the realities of life and death, which heighten our experience of loneliness. In adulthood, we begin to more fully understand our aloneness in the world. To deny our aloneness, we find ourselves in an endless pursuit of love and connection. Our cultural rituals, like weddings and birthday parties, provide opportunities for celebratory gatherings that help keep us connected. Religious organizations also serve as a way to feel part of a community with like-minded individuals.

When we lack a sense of community, our life choices can become negatively influenced, particularly by those we share our hearts with in an intimate relationship. We may be more likely to make impetuous decisions out of fear. The saying "opposites attract" points to the sparks that can fly when we meet someone different from us. When the initial attraction begins to wane and conflict arises, many people feel stuck; they don't want to be alone, but they don't know how to fix the issues. One of my clients, Ariana, struggled anytime she was single for more than a few months at a time. Since high school, she consistently dated and typically stayed in relationships longer than she knew she should, in order to avoid being alone. Despite being quite popular in high school and college, with a solid group of friends, she lived in fear of losing people from her life. Now in her 30s, she is in a relationship that could potentially lead to marriage. But her fears around their long-term compatibility are becoming harder to ignore or deny. She is conflicted about whether to continue in the relationship or end it in hopes of finding someone whose personality and values more closely align with hers.

Feelings that are heightened during our adolescent development, such as the fear of alienation from our peers or of getting left behind, tend to dissipate in adulthood. But if they continue to be strong, the desire for validation from external sources clouds judgment and compromises important life decisions. As the relationships we enter become more serious and the pressure regarding marriage begins, the stakes become higher. Cacioppo writes in *Loneliness*, "Even transient feelings that one is likely to face the future alone can increase the difficulty of self-regulation and ability to think clearly."

TOOLS FOR TREATING LONELINESS

The therapeutic approach shown to be the most effective in treating loneliness is Cognitive Behavioral Therapy (CBT). It is a solution-oriented treatment model based on the premise that our behavior is heavily influenced by our thoughts and that when we become more aware and directive of our thoughts, we can alter our behavior.

The typical steps of CBT treatment include:

- Identifying the current issues in your life you would like to change
- Becoming aware of your thoughts, emotions, and beliefs about these issues
- Identifying where there may be faulty thinking and replacing such thinking with a more objective and fair perspective.

There are a variety of exercises to guide the process of understanding why inaccurate beliefs exist and how to go about breaking ineffective thought patterns. The following is an example of one tool; additional exercises will be shared throughout the book.

Thought Diary:

1. Create a spreadsheet in your journal with the following column headers: *Emotion, Situation, Thoughts,* and *Alternative Thoughts.*

2. Each day, identify an uncomfortable emotion you experienced, such as anger, guilt, or anxiety, and rate the intensity of the feeling from 1 to 10.

3. In the *Situation* column, note what you were doing at the time, and under *Thoughts,* what you were saying to yourself that was probably unhelpful.

4. Write what you could have said to yourself that would have been helpful. For example, instead of thinking, "I always mess up when I talk to my boss," say, "I'm probably making the talk with my boss a bigger deal than it really is."

SELF-REFLECTION

You have learned how inherent our need is to feel connected to others and how our past relationships, particularly in childhood, continue to influence our perspective and behaviors in the present. Now would be a good time to pause and reflect a bit more deeply on your own experiences. You can respond to these questions simply by thinking through them on your own, by journaling, or by sharing with a friend or partner.

- Growing up, how did your family relate and engage with one another? How did you connect?
- Were you a tight-knit group or did it feel like there were favorites or cliques?
- Can you recall times when you felt excluded or left out of your family? How did you handle it?
- Were there expectations or rules about privacy, or were there no boundaries in place?

ATTACHMENT THEORY

Attachment theory came about from research by John Bowlby in the 1960s and 1970s on the relationship infants had with their primary caregiver. What was abundantly clear from the research was that in order to develop healthy social and emotional skills, an infant must have a trusting relationship with at least one primary caregiver. Extensive studies followed, including those by Mary Ainsworth, in which infants were observed playing as their parent left and returned to the room. The way in which the child responded to the absence and return of the parent has informed the different styles of attachment. If a child displayed the following characteristics, they were considered securely attached:

- The child wants to be with their parents versus strangers.
- They are able to separate from their parents without becoming very upset.
- The child is happy to see their parents when they return.
- They trust they can turn to their parents for comfort when afraid.

Subsequent research has applied this theory to our experience in relationships as adults, noting similarities that carry over from childhood. Our attachment style not only impacts the way in which we emotionally connect with our partners, but also contributes to what attracts us and keeps us in relationships or has us running from them. This psychological model provides evidence about our biological need for connection and how we learn to trust others, express our emotions, and handle the stress of being separated from those important to us. It also has contributed to our understanding of why we are all unique in how we interpret and experience our emotions.

The Four Attachment Styles

Outlined on the following pages are the four types of attachment: secure, anxious, avoidant, and disorganized. As you read through each description, note where you may identify with some of the beliefs or behavioral patterns. Also consider what may have influenced them, for example, childhood experiences, your unique temperament or personality, or past relationships. This is not about blame or skirting responsibility but about opening up to a greater understanding of yourself and those around you.

Secure: Adults who demonstrate good self-esteem and are comfortable sharing their feelings and asking for what they need. They can trust, support, and comfort their partners. They are able to see conflict as constructive and expect positive outcomes. The majority of people identify with this attachment; about 50 to 60 percent.

Anxious: Adults who struggle to see their self-worth and feel insecure. They very much want to experience love and intimacy, but their anxiety fosters clinginess and jealousy. They may seem to lose themselves in the relationship and neglect other life responsibilities. In order to keep their partners close, they feel they need to manipulate them through guilt or frequent confrontations when they feel threatened or ignored.

Avoidant: Adults who avoid emotional intimacy and often struggle to remain faithful in relationships. They may truly want to be in a relationship, but their lack of self-esteem and fear of how they may be engulfed or hurt in relationships propel them to build walls between themselves and their partners and to feel unsafe being completely vulnerable. They tend to be described as hot and cold, often sending mixed messages, and preferring casual relationships or casual sex.

Disorganized: Adults who find it extremely difficult to become close to others out of fear and lack of trust. They may identify as being shy or a loner. In times of conflict, they struggle to self-soothe or express their true needs to their partner. They may become aggressive, controlling, and turn to substances to cope.

Hopefully, you are able to recognize that you are not alone in the problems you have experienced in previous relationships. It is very important to remember, though, that these styles are not unchangeable. For my client Ariana, she typically identified her style as anxious, yet it was not consistent across the board in all of her romantic relationships. I often pointed out to her that her relationship in college had a very different dynamic compared to the relationship she was in at that moment. She had expressed feeling very safe and secure, even avoidant at times, but rarely anxious. This illustrates the fact that our attachment style is also influenced by the other person in the relationship and the way in which they attach.

GUIDED MEDITATION FOR GROUNDING AND RELAXATION

In moments of anxiety or stress, addressing the uncomfortable feelings instead of distracting yourself or numbing them not only helps quell them in the moment, but gradually decreases their severity over time. A helpful tool, particularly when feeling overwhelmed emotionally, is to do a grounding activity. The term grounding refers to feeling solidly rooted and anchored to the present moment. There are a variety of grounding techniques that are quite simple yet effective, such as listening to or singing the lyrics to your favorite song, naming the colors in the room you are in, or smelling aromatherapy oil. Guided meditation has also been found to be very supportive. The meditation below will help you feel more connected to your body in order to bring about a calming and peaceful state of mind.

- Begin in a comfortable position, either lying down or sitting.
- Tune in to your breath and notice any areas of tension in your body.
- Take full breaths, in through your nose and out through your mouth.
- Observe your body's response and try not to judge it.

CONTINUED >>

CONTINUED >>

- Take another breath, in and out, making your exhale longer than your inhale.
- Notice if it feels difficult to breathe deeply.
- Is your body feeling more relaxed or are there areas that are sore or tight?
- Are you feeling resistant to connecting with your body or your emotions?
- Are you able to easily focus on the breath or is your mind restless?
- Next, place your hands over your heart, and deeply breathe in and out.
- Say to yourself, "I am calm and at peace in this moment."
- Notice again your quality of mind and scan your body for areas of tension.
- Say to yourself, "I feel grounded and relaxed in this moment."
- Take the time you need to repeat these statements.
- When ready, gently open your eyes and observe your mental and physical state.

MINDFUL SELF-COMPASSION

Instead of mercilessly judging and criticizing yourself for various inadequacies or shortcomings, self-compassion means you are kind and understanding when confronted with personal failings—after all, who ever said you were supposed to be perfect?
—KRISTIN NEFF, PhD

A therapeutic approach that has also been widely effective in improving self-esteem and decreasing loneliness is Mindful Self-Compassion. It encourages directing the care and understanding we often give freely to others to ourselves as well. By learning how to respond and label challenging situations in a fair and considerate manner versus in a dismissive or critical way, we build greater emotional resilience. Self-compassion is measured according to three main elements:

Self-kindness versus self-judgment: When the reality of our humanness is accepted, we can respond with kindness to failures or shortcomings.
Common humanity versus isolation: Awareness of the fact that, as humans, we all suffer and are imperfect. When we resist this truth, we become frustrated and irrationally critical of ourselves for any inadequacy or vulnerability.

Mindfulness versus over-identification: Applying an open and curious mind-set to your thoughts and feelings will help bring about clarity and avoid suppressing them. Additionally, taking a step back and objectively looking at your problems relative to others who are also suffering will help you avoid becoming consumed or synonymous with your struggles.

When you regularly practice self-compassion, you will feel more balanced in your emotions and confidently take the steps necessary to cultivate the life you desire. Genuinely caring for and speaking to yourself in a kind manner is neither weak nor easy; it requires a motivated dedication toward shifting your mind-set.

COMMON RELATIONSHIP FEARS

Understandably, we want to avoid pain—
physical and emotional. Just as we learn to not
touch a hot stove after our first burn, we refrain
from things in our lives that may bring about emotional pain. Experiencing rejection or shame can
trigger a similar automatic response. In an effort
to protect ourselves from these feelings, we avoid
or move through our lives with extreme caution.
According to researcher Brené Brown, shame is
one of the most powerful emotions. At its core,
shame is the fear that we are not good enough.
Yet the measures we take to protect ourselves
from experiencing feelings such as judgment, criticism, or disappointment within our relationships
ultimately inhibit trust and vulnerability. Since it
is impossible to numb certain emotions and not
others, we end up numbing all emotions to some
degree along with other opportunities for growth
and deeper connection. Self-protective walls are
built and separate us from our partners.

In Susan Piver's book *The Wisdom of a Broken
Heart*, she addresses how difficult it is to navigate
the pain and grief after a breakup. Commonplace
advice is to move on or distract from the feelings.
After her own experience of healing from an ago-
nizing breakup, she states, "Why doesn't anyone
tell you that leaning into what terrifies you is far

more effective (and interesting) than doing everything in your power to escape it?" When we are willing to confront our fears, the reality of what we have been afraid of becomes less impossible to face and most often less catastrophic than our minds want us to believe.

RELATIONSHIP KILLERS

Intimate relationships are one of life's greatest sources of joy, but with them also come intense feelings that force us to face our inner demons around vulnerability. In a new relationship, it is natural to feel like you are on a roller coaster ride of connection and rejection, unable to see the next turn, drop, or flip. You may battle intense feelings of inadequacy and read into a normal event signs of potential trouble. Yet if the same intensity remains months in, an underlying insecurity is to blame and can wreak havoc on the relationship. Some of the common relationship killers include:

- Mind reading and catastrophizing—*"He hasn't texted in the last 10 minutes; he must be bored by me and is planning to dump me."*
- Need to control the relationship—*"I need to know for certain her feelings for me,"* and *"Tell me what you're thinking."*

- Fear of interdependence and space—*"We must spend all of our time together and have the same interests."*
- Comparing the new relationship to old ones— *"My ex cheated on me; it's just a matter of time before she does, too."*
- Relying on your partner for assurance—*"He must constantly tell me that he loves me and reassure me about my fears."*

Addressing your underlying fears, ideally prior to entering a relationship, will provide you with the capacity for greater self-assurance as you navigate intimacy and the challenges of vulnerability. Think back to your previous dating and relationship experiences, grab a journal, and write your responses to the following questions.

1. Which relationship killers, if any, have you experienced?
2. How have they impacted your current or past relationships?
3. What do you think triggered these fears?
4. What purpose do they serve? (They wouldn't be there if they didn't meet some need.)
5. If you are currently in a relationship, how could you go about communicating your fears in a different way?

CONCLUSION

In this chapter, we looked at how our past relationships significantly influence how we show up in our current relationships. Understanding attachment theory also hopefully helped you recognize where some of your or your partner's (current or past) problematic patterns originated. You cannot undo the past, but you can take steps toward compassionately redirecting yourself out of unhealthy dynamics. If we can make peace with old relationships, forgiving others and ourselves, we can make meaning of the relationship instead of allowing it to keep us stuck in resentment, anger, and fear. As you step around these fears, you become more present and genuine, allowing for more authentic connections and lasting relationships.

AFFIRMATIONS

I am worthy of having my needs respected
by others.

I do not allow fear to dictate my life.

I let go of the desire to change the past.

I treat others in the ways I want to be treated.

I value myself and my time and spend it on
things that nourish me.

Don't surrender your loneliness so quickly.
Let it cut more deeply.
Let it ferment and season you as few humans
or even divine ingredients can.
—HAFIZ

CHAPTER 3

You Are Worthy of Love

This chapter will encourage you to look more closely at the thoughts and beliefs you have about yourself. The dialogue in our minds dictates our experiences and is a significant contributing factor to our feelings of loneliness. If you are intensely critical of yourself, your ability to take risks and try new things will feel even more enervating. Difficult emotions become magnified when we judge ourselves harshly, especially while pursuing love. Doing whatever you can to avoid this self-criticism makes sense (i.e., by avoiding risk-taking), yet the end result is a life that feels unfulfilled. In life, as in love, we are all called to follow our own compass and, at times, take the road less traveled. Possessing a strong sense of self enables a person to take those leaps of faith, trusting that however painful the landing may be, they will get back up and move forward, stronger.

BETTER SELF-ESTEEM = BETTER RELATIONSHIPS

Your self-esteem is based on your inherent sense of value or self-worth. If you feel confident in yourself and believe in your abilities, your relationships and other facets of your life such as your work, finances, and health stand to benefit. If you have too little self-esteem, opportunities and risks become harder to pursue. You are more likely to have loose boundaries and tolerate poor treatment from others. On the other hand, if you have too much self-esteem or an inflated ego, you may alienate yourself from others with a sense of entitlement or inability to admit when you are wrong. As with most things, your self-esteem fluctuates throughout your life, especially during challenging times like a breakup or loss of a job. Improving your self-esteem will be tantamount to creating lasting change in the care and keeping of fulfilling relationships.

Relationship with Self

The type of relationship you have with yourself outweighs the impact that both your current and past relationships with others have on your experience of loneliness. The power and influence of our self-talk account for why a successful billionaire can feel insecure and like an imposter, while her administrative assistant can feel fulfilled, prosperous, and worthy. It all boils down to how we talk to and perceive ourselves. It is to be expected that someone will experience low points in their life, which may translate to low points in their self-esteem, especially during periods of numerous transitions (e.g., adolescence). It's also quite natural to have an ebb and flow in one's self-confidence across varied aspects of identity. For example, your confidence in your professional identity may be very high; even if you drop the ball on something, you trust your ability to think critically and fix the situation. Your self-concept in dating, though, might feel low; you may struggle just to send a text or question every move you make, not trusting that you are good enough. If you have recently gone through a breakup or have been single for a while, your confidence may be lower.

It is helpful to recognize these dips as a normal part of life transitions, inspiring hope and faith that your negative self-concept will improve. If your self-esteem is something you have struggled with consistently since childhood, the stories and exercises in this chapter will help you let go of the beliefs you've held on to that are no longer serving you.

HOW TO AMPLIFY YOUR CONFIDENCE WHILE DATING

The trouble is not that I am single and likely to stay single, but that I am lonely and likely to stay lonely.
—CHARLOTTE BRONTË

It is no wonder that dating can do a number on a person's self-esteem. With each failed text exchange, date, or relationship, your self-worth can take a nosedive into self-reproach. By changing your attitude, and integrating the tenets described here, you can enjoy more of the highs than the lows of the dating experience.

1. **Bring an open-minded, lighthearted spirit to your search.** You are not figuring out a life-or-death nuclear code—you are exploring who's a good match. There's no need to be so serious or stoic about the process. Let yourself enjoy and be open to possibilities and new opportunities for growth and learning.

2. **Face old fears.** Your past negative experiences will continue to affect your future ones if you do not recognize the stories they have created in your mind regarding safety, trust, or your value. Journaling and talking it out with friends or a therapist will help you release these fears and open yourself up to a new experience.

3. **Reject rejection.** Being broken up with or "ghosted" by someone can easily turn into a story of self-blame or judgment. Reframing it as "we were not right for each other" puts no one in the wrong and helps you move on.

4. **Let go of the timeline.** Pressure, impatience, and socially or personally imposed urgency do not create the space for curiosity, fun, and the ability to be present and mindful.

5. **You are complete right now.** Yes, you may want to be in a loving relationship—most people do—but pursuing that does not make you any less of a complete or whole person.

WHAT MAKES YOU *YOU*

Many of us consistently dismiss our personal strengths in favor of focusing on our weaknesses in order to potentially fix or mitigate them. Out of our need for connection, we focus on how we are perceived by others, cultivating what we believe are the "right" external characteristics and downplaying our natural, intrinsic qualities, like humility, curiosity, or empathy. If connecting authentically with others is your goal, focusing on what you can naturally contribute to the relationship will help boost your confidence. This exercise is meant to help you balance your list of weaknesses by acknowledging the traits and qualities that make you unique.

- Make a list of your strengths, writing them out as complete sentences. For example, "People have told me I am a good listener."
- Choose three traits to make into positive affirmations, for example, "I am a good listener," and write them on sticky notes.
- Place the notes on a mirror, in your calendar, or near your desk.

BE POSITIVE ABOUT WHO YOU ARE

When a person is secure in their self-worth, they have the capacity to enter into a relationship as their authentic selves. If they wrestle with accepting who they are, self-protective patterns develop out of fear of inevitable rejection. For example, if someone struggles with running from relationships just as they are becoming serious, their conscious or unconscious fear could be telling them that if they stay, it will become more difficult to hide the parts of themselves they do not want seen. They might also look for flaws in their partner while battling with their own harsh judgments of themselves. If one or both partners struggle with seeing the good in themselves, their judgment will create an invisible wall between them, regardless of the love that exists. I have witnessed this time and again with clients who for years have worn an invisible mask in order to keep their struggle with self-worth hidden from those they love.

My client Jack stated that his goal for therapy was to improve his approach to meeting someone, as online dating had only resulted in uncomfortable first dates or meaningless sex. Jack wanted to find someone he could be himself with and craved the comfort and support of a committed relationship. At 36, he was struggling with profound loneliness after the end of his marriage two years previously. Jack remained friends with his ex-wife and she had recently shared with him that she was engaged. He was happy for her but felt even more pressure to move on and feared falling behind his peers. Jack often remarked how lucky he was to have been married to someone like his wife and had many regrets around how he had behaved in the relationship. To escape these thoughts, he was turning to food and marijuana more and more, resulting in weight gain and poor body image. Each week in our sessions, Jack expressed how lonely he felt, particularly during the weekends, feeling paralyzed and unable to reach out to his friends and family.

Even though the weekends spent mostly at home alone were triggering his loneliness, scheduling activities was not the solution. On the nights when he would go out with friends, he often ended up feeling even more disconnected and critical of himself. It was clear that healing his loneliness meant more than just seeking out companionship. Jack was also cognizant of the fact that even when he was married and felt loved by his wife and accepted by his peers, he struggled with feelings of inadequacy and a desire to avoid social gatherings. As our work progressed, Jack came to realize that the relationship he truly needed to work on was the one he had with himself.

Self-Worth

In our pursuit of connection and acceptance, we can get caught up in an endless cycle of seeking out external validation. We do this because it makes us feel that we are more in control of our lives, gaining bits of proof of our value and worth. We also tend to believe that once we become the ideal version of ourselves or obtain something we want (e.g., a new job, home, or level of income), we will finally feel good about who we are and be respected by others. Those accomplishments can foster feelings of pride and satisfaction, but they are unfortunately impermanent. Investing your effort, time, and money in pursuing these brief highs of happiness results in your day-to-day life being overshadowed by a sense of lack. Instead, dedicating your time to the things that truly matter to you and give you joy will bring about greater long-term rewards in your self-worth. In his book *The Seat of the Soul*, Gary Zukav posits, "Power is the alignment of your personality with your soul.

When personality serves the energy of your soul, that is authentic empowerment." By focusing your attention on what is more in alignment with your unique talents or interests, your soul will be treated to a five-course meal versus just dessert. You will feel a deeper sense of contentment and balance when facing the highs and lows of life.

Another worthwhile way of building your self-worth is giving back and being of service to others. The American philosopher Ralph Waldo Emerson said, "The purpose of life is not to be happy. It is to be useful, to be honorable, to be compassionate, to have it make some difference that you have lived and lived well." By acknowledging your innate and unique strengths, you tap into ways of contributing to the world as well as bringing more purpose and meaning to your life. For Jack, as he realized the degree to which his intense self-judgment was triggering his loneliness and keeping him from connecting to those around him, he committed himself to shifting his mind-set by stepping out of his comfort zone. Always a lover of dogs, Jack decided to volunteer at his local animal shelter. He enjoyed taking the dogs on walks and could feel the appreciation from them as well as the staff. As Jack's ability to acknowledge his positive traits became easier, his desire to numb his emotions decreased significantly. Gradually, Jack was able to decrease the power the old childhood stories had over him and instead focus more on the present, recognizing and taking in the moments in which he felt accepted and appreciated by his family, friends, peers, and colleagues.

If one does not claim their innate sense of worth and grow it in real and meaningful ways, the desire for validation will constantly be sought from others. They will also be drawn to ways in which they can be distracted or numbed from the pain of feeling unworthy. Instead, by practicing self compassion, one creates the space to recognize the good in themselves and the worthiness of their life, without having to prove or earn it.

VALUES ASSESSMENT

One way to help you determine where to dedicate your time is to reassess your values. Our values are guiding principles for our thoughts and actions. When we do not act in accordance with them, our life will feel out of balance and lack meaning. As you answer the following questions, consider the actions you can take to improve your self-worth now versus in the future.

- What do you value in your life? Try to acknowledge at least five things. For instance, spending time with family, success at your job, living in a big city or small town, having a stable income, a hobby, or ability to travel.
- What has influenced your values?
- Do your values feel rigid or flexible?
- Are there areas or times in your life when you've had to compromise your values?
- Do your values feel attainable or do they feel out of reach? (Are they realistic?)

Go through your list and assign a percentage according to the general amount of time you currently dedicate to that value. For example: family, 30 percent; work, 50 percent; learning/reading, 10 percent; travel, 10 percent. I often draw out a pie chart with my clients to help visualize the breakdown.

- In which areas do you feel content and which ones would you like to adjust? Rewrite the percentages based on your preference, while considering the current circumstances of your life that may be out of your control.
- What are the concrete steps you need to take now and in the future in order to live more aligned with your values?

ACCEPT YOUR EMOTIONS

Accepting yourself goes hand in hand with accepting your emotions. How you understand and respond to your emotions is central to living your life authentically. It is a continual process, checking in with yourself and being attuned to whatever is happening inside your mind and body. Some emotions may be very familiar and others surprisingly new. It may take just a few seconds, but learning to actually feel what you feel can change your life. It's okay to surrender to whatever is happening inside your mind and body. By and large, fighting how you feel or trying to cover it up will make it worse.

Burying emotions does not erase them. One of the strongest emotions at the root of low self-esteem is unresolved anger. For example, the pain we experienced as a result of unmet needs during our childhood becomes lodged within us. We learn to blame ourselves or to push down the anger and resentment toward our caregivers in fear of alienating ourselves even further. As we grow into adults, the anger that simmers beneath may show up as guardedness or hostility, contributing to loneliness and disconnection.

You may have people in your life who make you feel invalidated, angry, or belittled. Often, instead of addressing the impact of their words or actions, we try to avoid future hurts by walking on eggshells around them, staying hyper-focused on their needs and emotions versus our own. Yet this avoidance contributes to disconnection and the dissolution of relationships. By prioritizing how you feel, regardless of whether it is accepted, understood, or acknowledged by others, you honor yourself and create the potential to heal the relationship.

LET GO OF CONTROL

One of the most common human desires is to feel in control. We attempt to plan out our lives and avoid problems or errors as much as possible. We also prefer that the people in our lives think and act the way we do. But the reality is that we have very little control. You can't control why your Tinder matches keep ghosting you or why your ex decided to break up with you. You can, however, control how you choose to react to these situations. Understandably, this fact of life can trigger anxiety and fear of the unknown. One way of resisting this is by using manipulation tactics in order to get what we want. This may look like shaming someone for not believing in the same thing as you or withdrawing affection in order to get them to do what you want.

YOUR SILVER LININGS

Recall a challenging experience in your life that you did not expect to turn out well, but did. One where it was difficult to see the light at the end of the tunnel while in the midst of the experience.

- How did you cope prior to knowing how it would turn out? How did you manage your feelings?
- Had you considered the positive outcome as a possibility?
- If not, what do you think stopped you from considering such an outcome? For example, fear of hoping for something and not getting it (disappointment), or fear that it may make you more vulnerable to judgment (self-protection)?
- Can you recall how you responded to the outcome? In gratitude or was it regarded as a fluke?
- Have you come to realize that you learned something from the experience, or that it served you in some other unexpected way?

MIND GAMES

Our minds often play tricks on us, creating false or illogical patterns of thinking. It does so in order to protect us from potential danger, yet it typically results in more harm than good. If we allow the games to play out, our thoughts are dictated by a feedback loop of worry, anxiety, and trepidation. CBT labels these types of thoughts as cognitive distortions. By learning to identify these unproductive ways of thinking, you can begin to respond to them objectively. As you read a few of the most common distortions described here, consider a current issue you are having and which distortion(s) you may be succumbing to. It can be very helpful to write out the thought or belief, name the distortion, and then identify a more rational and fair perspective.

- Black-and-white thinking: looking at things as either/or, in the extremes, struggling to find the middle ground.
- Personalization: believing you are the cause of other people's negative emotions.
- Overgeneralizing: focusing on one piece of evidence and generalizing it to an overall pattern, typically about yourself or your environment.
- Jumping to conclusions: determining that one piece of evidence points to a certain belief as fact.
- Magnification (catastrophizing) or minimization: exaggerating or minimizing the importance or meaning of things.

Another way that our desire for control manifests is through perfectionism. Interpretations of perfectionism vary but it is often regarded as a positive trait; representative of someone who is hardworking and fastidious. However, what drives this trait is not simply a desire to do well, but an effort to prove oneself or cover up inadequacy. For example, believing that if you were just able to look and act perfectly, life would improve, and your loneliness would decrease. It can become a form of armor, an attempt to block out judgment or blame. Instead, it keeps someone locked in a pattern of calculated actions and intense self-criticism. That perfectionism is so pervasive points to the fact that, to some degree, it works, and does bring about success. Yet the ability to actually enjoy the success is short-lived as the perfectionistic mind-set will quickly find the next thing to improve upon.

In order to find peace within ourselves around the desire for control and acceptance from others, there are several evidence-based tools that can help retrain the brain. In the next chapter, I will detail how you can apply these to your life. They include:

Empathy: The ability to consider another person's perspective without judgment.

Self-compassion: Responding to yourself with kindness when encountering struggle or failure.

Radical acceptance: Letting go of expecting things to be a certain way and accepting what is.

THE BENEFITS OF A POSITIVE OUTLOOK

Loneliness is a subjective feeling and is based on the interpretation of an experience. Akin to the positive effects of placebos, what we think about something impacts our emotional and physical response. As you navigate life's highs and lows, such as during a difficult breakup or when at your wit's end about online dating, the perspective you decide to take will impact your ability to heal and move on. Maintaining a pessimistic attitude is like being tied to an anchor in a deep sea of negativity and hopelessness. There is a part of you that wants something better, but fear keeps you from trusting it could happen, creating an internal struggle. Do not take this to mean that you should never allow yourself to be angry or frustrated. There are things that happen in life that have no positive spin on them. But choosing a positive frame of mind does not mean being blind to the unjust realities of life. If you want to make changes and let go of pain from your past, altering your perspective will help you untether yourself from that pain.

Cognitive diffusion is a technique that can help bring about neutrality or give you space from your thoughts. By acknowledging potentially harmful, repetitive thoughts through labeling them, you can remove their power. For example, you can work on changing the thought "I am a failure" to "I am *thinking* that I am a failure." This will give you the opportunity to question the thought to determine if it is truly based in fact. Further, by reframing distressing experiences, focusing instead on the parts that were good or what you learned from them, allows your mind and heart to be free, versus heavy with regret and pain. Believing in your capacity to grow and evolve makes meaning out of the past and brings hope for the future. You have the power to change the course of your life. With each experience, you grow, getting closer to knowing and accepting your true self.

THE POWER OF VISUALIZATION

Your most treasured memories are often tied to specific feelings you can reexperience by closing your eyes and visualizing. Just as you can reconnect with feelings from the past, your day-to-day life is also impacted subconsciously by your thoughts and feelings related to the immediate and distant future. If you become more aware of this connection, you can harness the power to make your experiences in the present and future more in line with what you want. Many successful athletes, performers, and leaders extoll the benefits of visualization. Several best-selling books have been written on the topic, yet it remains a relatively untapped resource. The technique posits that by allowing yourself to see in your mind the things that you want, you allow your body to feel the positive feelings that would arise if those visions were true. It is like laying tracks in your mind for the possibility of whatever you would like to call into your life.

CONTINUED >>

CONTINUED >>

1. Visualization can take place anywhere, but it is ideal to do it in a calm setting; for instance, a favorite room in your house or a quiet corner of a park.
2. Initially, in order to help calm your mind, it may be helpful to determine a set length of time, for instance, allocating two minutes to visualize each morning or evening.
3. Sit in a comfortable position and softly close your eyes.
4. You can place one hand on your heart and the other on your stomach to help connect your mind and body.
5. Begin to think about what it is you would like to have or do in your life. Create a picture in your mind of what that would look like. Visualize as many details as you can.
6. As you do so, cultivate a feeling of openness and positivity, fully believing that this could be your reality. Having a smile on your face can be very helpful in blocking resistance or self-criticism.
7. End with a positive statement around your deservingness or self-worth, perhaps choosing one of the affirmations found within this book.

CONCLUSION

In this chapter, you learned how your self-esteem impacts not only your loneliness but your overall quality of life. You were encouraged in the reflection exercises to identify your strengths and the traits that make you unique. Additionally, you were asked to get clear on your values and how much time you are currently dedicating to them. The detrimental impact of perfectionism and desire for control were explored as well as the more meaningful and long-term benefits of providing acts of service and tapping in to your natural talents. Lastly, the power of positive thinking and visualizations were also shared as tools toward creating the life that you want.

AFFIRMATIONS

I choose to live my life in accordance
with my values.

I am able to let go of things that
are outside of my control.

I believe in the power of a
positive outlook.

I am needed, valued, and
appreciated by others.

Solitude is fine, but you need someone to
tell you that solitude is fine.
–HONORÉ DE BALZAC

Loneliness is the poverty of self;
solitude is the richness of self.
–MAY SARTON

CHAPTER 4

Embracing Solitude

Even more important than the steps you take to deepen your connection with others is your ability to be alone with yourself. When you feel safe being alone with your thoughts, the internal dialogues that occur are potential catalysts for growth, healing, and transformation. Given the space to be heard, your intuition will guide you toward greater contentment and peace. Yet for many, spending time alone without any form of distraction feels torturous. To avoid this dis-comfort, we choose to spend time with people who are not good for us, overwork ourselves to the point of burnout, or get lost in the world of technology to pass the hours in the day. All of this points to the fact that being alone is not the problem. It is our reaction to being alone that must be addressed.

LONELINESS VS. SOLITUDE

Solitude, like loneliness, is subjective. It requires that a person be alone, but the perspective they have on that experience informs the difference. Writer and philosopher Paul Tillich said, "Loneliness expresses the pain of being alone and solitude expresses the glory of being alone." When a person loses the ability to enjoy being alone and links the experience entirely to one of loneliness, it is understandable that they will do whatever they can to avoid it. Alternatively, accepting that aloneness is not only tolerable but necessary will reveal the gifts of solitude.

The option of choice is another significant difference between loneliness and solitude. Solitude requires a conscious decision to embrace and enjoy time spent alone. When experiencing loneliness, one is rejecting the present moment and longing for something else. With technology now at our fingertips in a multitude of ways, it can be so easy to distract oneself from loneliness by going online. Yet by and large, it does little to feed the need for connection and can lead to even greater loneliness. While in solitude, you are resourcing your mind and body, attuning to your own completeness. Research has shown that carving out time for solitude improves health in a variety of ways. Just as medical advice commonly recommends exercise and a balanced diet, so too is it important that we develop and learn to appreciate time alone, to improve the functioning of the mind and body. In her book *Alone Together*, Sherry Turkle, director of the MIT Initiative on Technology and Self, suggests that "people should be mindfully setting aside chunks of every day when they are not engaged in so-called social snacking activities like texting, g-chatting, and talking on the phone." Prioritizing quality time with others over the quantity of time will also result in improvements to your social life. Balancing your time with and without others can contribute to more enjoyment of each experience. Taking breaks to recharge and relax increases your capacity to be mindful and engaged. Further, knowing that you have carved out time for yourself to attend to other life responsibilities enables you to be less distracted and on edge when you're with others.

Experiencing painful rejection from peers or a significant other will understandably cause resistance toward being alone. But allowing yourself to be with the feelings can bring about clarity and inspiration. From her research on social rejection, Sharon Kim, assistant professor at Johns Hopkins University, found that experiencing social rejection can lead to greater creativity and ingenuity: "The experience of rejection may trigger a psychological process that stimulates, rather than stifles, performance on creative tasks." The fact that many of the great thinkers and artists of history, such as Isaac Newton and Beethoven, were known to have spent much of their time alone further proves this finding.

Potential benefits of solitude include:
- Improved focus and productivity
- Increased capacity for empathy for others
- Improved mood
- A sense of freedom
- Greater connection to spirituality
- Increased memory
- A greater sense of self-empowerment
- Freedom from self-consciousness around others
- Greater connection to nature

MOMENTS OF SOLITUDE

Can you call to mind times in your life when you enjoyed or craved time alone? It may have been while on vacation, becoming engrossed in a new activity or hobby, or simply going for an evening stroll. Picture yourself in those moments.

- What made it feel okay to be alone?
- Did you experience positive feelings associated with solitude? If so, what were they?
- Can you reserve time each day for solitude? Regardless of whether it is three minutes or three hours, practice becoming more comfortable with sanctioned time to be alone.

YOU ARE YOUR BEST COMPANY

In spite of the many benefits of solitude, societal judgment of it remains. There is an unspoken expectation that each person should be able to discover what they are passionate about, act on their intuition, and feel fulfilled, all the while doing so in the constant company of others. I understand that, depending on how lonely you feel right now, believing you are your own best company may feel unbearable. If so, I ask that you allow this as a possibility and see it more as a future-oriented goal.

After reading chapter 3, you may have become clearer on how you see yourself and the impact your judgment has on your relationship with loneliness. Naturally, one would be inclined to decrease loneliness by focusing on ways to better connect with others. But improving the way you relate to yourself keeps the feeling of loneliness at bay much more than filling your time with the company of others. When you feel at home with yourself, you conserve the energy that is drained when seeking safety and acceptance in others. You find that you crave your own company, as it feels nourishing and dependable instead of tenuous and conditional. However, no matter how great your relationship is with yourself, the feeling of lacking to some degree will never fully disappear.

As with loneliness, feeling a deficiency indicates a need for something, a change, or evidence of a constricted viewpoint. This can often be where our egos show up and distract us from our intuition and faith. Our ego wants us to fit in, succeed, and excel, but it does so by motivating us out of fear versus love. Fear more easily takes over when we are confused and do not feel grounded in ourselves. Without a foundation of self-love, the fear of lacking breeds greater disconnection and insecurity. It is often the cause of the "drama" in our lives we say we want to avoid. Our ego loves to place the blame entirely on others or go to the other extreme and hold ourselves fully responsible for any and all conflicts or problems, filling us with guilt and shame. By prioritizing solitude, we strengthen the relationship we have with ourselves and improve our ability to address our needs and desires without allowing the ego to take over.

Enjoy This Time on Your Own

If you have recently gone through a breakup, have been single for several years, or have never been in a relationship, the fear that you may be

WHEN DO YOU FEEL JOY?

In order to decrease your loneliness, you will need to add to your life, and why not make it something that brings you joy? Answer the following questions.

- What are the things you do in your life that you truly enjoy?
- When do you feel free, most alive, or connected to yourself?
- What keeps you from committing more time to doing the things you enjoy?
- Over the course of one week, try to track the moments you felt happy or joyful.

alone forever may feel nagging and unrelenting. As much as it would make life easier to know when the next relationship will be, we must surrender to the unknown of this important aspect of our lives. Yet our ego's desire for control can lead us to believe we are solely at fault for our relationship status and encourage us to try to take matters into our own hands. You can attempt to live in hiding until you are no longer single, place the things that bring you joy on hold until your next relationship, and make dating or waiting your number one priority. Or you can choose a different perspective. You could recognize that being single provides you with freedom; freedom to focus on whatever makes you happy, without having to compromise or concern yourself with another's needs or opinions. Focusing on yourself does not make you selfish. To the contrary, making the most of this time and enjoying it on your own will support you in your growth toward becoming the person you want to be, for yourself, for those you love, and for those you will eventually love.

Honor this time alone by regularly reassessing and refining your life's dreams, passions, and goals. Just as taking the time to adjust the lens on a camera allows the image to become more focused, dedicating this undefined time of being single to becoming clear on the life you want for yourself in the next 5, 10, or 20 years will keep you closer to the path that will get you there. If you tend to run from these types of life decisions or prefer to leave them up to someone else, recognize that these are common forms of self-sabotage. Sitting with and surrendering to the discomfort of the unknown precedes positive change. Being patient with yourself will help you avoid rash decisions or giving up altogether and returning to known yet unfulfilling patterns of behavior. Enjoying this time on your own will allow you to avert the circular paths that delay, distract, or confuse you from moving in the direction you want to go.

Remember, you are in charge of your life and no one is free from making mistakes or feeling stuck. You learn life's lessons as you experience them, from your successes and, even more so, your failures. As a child, you most likely felt freer to voice what you liked and didn't, and were more open to exploration, creativity, and fun. As adults, our commitments and relationships infringe upon our ability to be as carefree and expressive as we once were. We must find ways to preserve our sense of freedom in order to avoid feeling trapped, controlled, or unfulfilled. Claiming your freedom while alone will be beneficial to you now as well as long into the future.

USING THE REARVIEW MIRROR TO DRIVE (BUT ONLY FOR A BIT)

Breaks in relationships are also a good time to take stock of your life and consider new opportunities or goals. As a young adult, you may have been encouraged or directed to create a post–high school life plan.

This may have entailed finding a job with which to support yourself or going to a college that would allow you to graduate with a degree in the field that interested you or was considered worthwhile. Take some time to examine what went into this decision-making process for you.

- Was it fueled by fear, other people's expectations, or your own interests?
- Are there things you wish you could have done differently?
- If you were someone who changed majors or career paths, do you think allowing yourself more time to consider what you truly wanted would have made a difference, or was it purely a result of learning as you went?
- What advice would you have given your teenage or twentysomething self, and could you possibly follow any of it today?

GET COMFORTABLE WITH BEING ALONE

Changing your mind-set on what it means to be alone is key, but following through with behavioral actions is also an important step toward decreasing loneliness. Even though we may think that starting or stopping something will be good for us, our physical reaction to that new or different thing can cause a fight, flight, or freeze response. By and large, we crave what is known and comfortable. When we do commit to something new or take a risk, it usually involves the support of another person. In order to become more comfortable being alone, you will need to guide or even trick your mind into not rushing to the panic button 10 minutes in. Learning a new hobby, going to an exercise class, or meditating are all activities that can get you used to doing things on your own.

When someone is single, they may throw themselves into serial dating and app swiping to avoid being alone. While this may alleviate some feelings of loneliness and potentially lead to a new partner, it can also backfire, particularly if the dates do not go well. Alternatively, someone may put dating on the back burner and instead make their career their priority. Our work relationships can be very beneficial to our well-being, yet can also create a false sense of connection. Often, if someone leaves a job, the link they had in common is gone and the relationship fades away. Additionally, because of the amount of time spent at work, expending the energy to meet people outside of the office can feel more trying. It is therefore important to balance out your time at work, dating, and managing other responsibilities with activities you enjoy doing on your own.

At 32, Evie sought out therapy to address her anxiety around never having been in a relationship. She was an extremely smart, funny, and attractive woman with a successful career in the restaurant industry. Her life was filled with work, and she loved it. Even on her days off, she was either at the restaurant or in contact with her team by email and text. Evie had several friends outside of work, yet she struggled to stay in regular contact with them and rarely was she the one to initiate when they did get together. She was also experiencing growing tension with her family and, even though they lived in a nearby city, they saw each other just on holidays and birthdays. Evie did not like the version of herself she had become: anxious and unable to slow down and relax. Even her work friends began joking about how stressed or tense she seemed.

Instead of jumping right in to dating to address her goal of being in a relationship, I encouraged Evie to take stock of her day-to-day life in order to become clear on where she could make room for dating and what she would need to let go of. Initially, it was very difficult for her to say anything disparaging about her work, but as she became more observant of the dynamics, she noticed the cracks in the foundation that she was too afraid to see before. She also came to realize that the colleagues at work who felt like family were not the people she believed would have her back when she needed support, and that she didn't feel she could be completely honest or herself around them. Gradually, Evie was able to decrease her time at work and commit to hobbies she used to enjoy, like swimming. She could also honor that this time being alone had given her the opportunity to dedicate herself to growing in her career and, now, to freely decide to step back from it and discover new interests.

AM I TOO COMFORTABLE BEING ALONE?

If you are wondering why you particularly don't mind being alone, but desire to feel less lonely, you are not the only one. Our temperaments can strongly impact our ability to withstand being alone and even the degree to which we feel lonely. It is not always black and white, but most people lean more toward being either more of an introvert or more of an extrovert. If my clients aren't sure where they fall, I ask them which scenario tends to energetically refuel them: a night alone at home or spending several hours at a social gathering? Historically, introverts have been given a hard time due to their reserve and solitary preferences. Yet recent research is changing this negative perception. In her book *Quiet: The Power of Introverts in a World That Can't Stop Talking*, Susan Cain observes, "Introversion is my greatest strength. I have such a strong inner life that I'm never bored and only occasionally lonely. No matter what mayhem is happening around me, I know I can always turn inward." If you identify as an introvert, seeing your strengths will help you get clarity on potentially different ways in which to address your loneliness. Going out to a bunch of social events will most likely not be the answer. What your loneliness may be signaling is a need for greater depth or authenticity in your current relationships or that more time is needed to grieve the end of past relationships. As you consider how to go about creating deeper bonds, think about the person with whom you feel the most refueled. What traits does that person possess or how do you show up in that relationship? Can you increase your time with this person? Are there ways you can transfer some of these aspects to other relationships?

Quiet Your Inner Critic

Many people hate being alone because they end up having to endure intense self-criticism that plays on repeat in their head. The inner critic is that voice inside you that picks apart your decisions and dwells on what went wrong in the past and what could go wrong in the future. It takes you out of the present moment and removes the possibility of feeling content. You learned in chapter 3 that when a person has positive self-esteem, they are able to better navigate life's highs and lows. This is not to say that they do not hit roadblocks in their lives; they do, just like everyone else. One of the differences, though, is that when they hit a roadblock, they are able to get back up, address the issue, and learn from it much more quickly.

When someone is overly self-critical, they will beat themselves up and get stuck ruminating on the what-ifs. Hence the saying "We are our own worst enemies." Allowing that voice too much airplay with free reign to comment on every experience may understandably cause one to stick with what's familiar in order to avoid potential missteps. Yet doing so leads to a life that is "safely disconnected," stuck in routine out of fear. The internal critic can also extend outward and negatively impact those around us, for example, by being overly competitive or needing to be right all of the time. Alternatively, a person may believe that everything that goes wrong around them is their fault and apologize profusely for any issue they perceive as their mistake.

The critical voice can become so ingrained that it may feel quite implausible to believe that this voice is not you. Take a moment now to consider the amount of time you judge yourself throughout the day. What percentage of your day do you spend critiquing yourself? Imagine if you were able to decrease that percentage by half, what might change in your life? Ignoring or quieting that voice may feel impossible, but I assure you it is not. One way to diminish its power is to empower the other parts or voices within that are more supportive and fair. I will often encourage my clients to consider how they would speak to a child or a good friend who was experiencing something they were going through. Would they tell them to shut up and grow up, or point out what an idiot they are? Absolutely not! By looking at it from this perspective, they are able to see how ridiculously harsh that voice is and how they would never speak to others in the way they speak to themselves.

Imagine if you went through life with the encouraging words of a kind friend in your ear. What could potentially change in how you see yourself or engage with others? Often some fear arises when I pose this question to my clients. Many express apprehension and concern that if they were kinder to themselves, they would become lazy, unsuccessful, or disconnected from reality. This was the case with my client Carin. As a successful woman in her early 30s, Carin loved her job, the city she lived in, and had a very active social life. She sought out therapy to address the fact that she had not been in a serious relationship since college. Her youngest sister had just gotten engaged and she was feeling hyper-aware of being single and feeling like she was falling behind her peers. It became apparent that Carin regarded socializing as something she "should" be doing and was closely linked to her identity as a friendly, busy, and outgoing person. She often had something planned every night of the week and would become frustrated with friends if they canceled at the last minute. To her surprise, I recommended that she decrease the number of events on her schedule and spend more time alone. She pushed back. Wouldn't she feel worse if she were sitting at home by herself? She also referenced a time in her past when, between ending and starting a new job, the lack of structure caused such intense anxiety that she turned to food and alcohol to an excessive degree. Understandably, she feared that this would happen again. As we worked through her concerns around slowing down and being perceived as lazy, she gradually began to block out time for herself to be alone. Her critical voice cried out in self-reproach, but as her energy level and self-esteem improved, she could more easily dismiss it and enjoy a greater sense of peace and self-acceptance than ever before.

Breaking free from your inner critic may still feel impossible. In spite of the abuse, it is what you are used to, and it has been beneficial in your life to some degree. Another technique I use with my clients to support them in separating from their critic is to regard it as a personal coach, one who resides in their head all day, every day. It can be even more helpful to visualize them, perhaps as a mean coach from their youth or someone in the media whose opinions are vastly different from their own. I explain that they have the option to either stick with the same coach they've had for years or try out a new one, and that they can always go back to the old coach whenever they want. The difference between the two is their strategies. Your current coach's tactic is to tear you down in order to motivate you toward obtaining success, happiness, and the respect of others. Alternatively, the new coach uses positive reinforcement and self-compassion to reach these same goals. If you knew for sure both coaches could get you to where you'd like to be, which one would you choose to guide you there?

STRATEGIES FOR QUIETING THE MIND

Countering your critical voice is hard work. To avoid burnout from challenging old ways of thinking, you can begin to incorporate a variety of activities to create peace in your mind. For example, developing a ritual of having a cup of tea in the afternoon can bring about a sense of calm and a break from spinning thoughts. Engaging in mindful stretching to start each day can be a wonderful way to increase oxygen to your brain and decrease morning jitters. Or during your daily commute, engaging in deep breathing can help connect you to your body as you transition from home to work and back again. Following are a few more ideas, but I encourage you to create your own list. Not all may work for you, or work every time, but they will support you in fending off burnout. They also support you in decreasing the mind-body symptoms of loneliness noted in chapter 1.

- Spend time in nature
- Get a massage
- Diffuse essential oils
- Cook a new recipe
- Listen to calming music
- Spend time with an animal
- Take a nap
- Take a bath or shower
- Turn off or disable phone alerts
- Skip the afternoon caffeine kick
- Paint, draw, or color
- Journal whatever comes to mind
- Watch a funny movie or video

GRATITUDE PRACTICE

A powerful way to shift your perspective is to begin a gratitude practice. By regularly acknowledging the things in your life that you are grateful for, you train your mind to focus on the good things more than the bad, and experience positive feelings. As your practice continues, your ability to notice the beauty in everyday life will grow. Particularly during difficult times in your life, maintaining a gratitude practice will support you in finding a sense of balance and hope. Here are some suggestions for how to begin, but there is no one right way; determine what feels doable for you.

- Use a blank journal, the Notes app on your phone, or find a gratitude journal that includes prompts.
- Acknowledge at least three things you are grateful for.
- Designate a time of day; usually first thing in the morning or end of day is best.
- Set an alarm on your phone to remind you to do this each day.
- Reach out to a friend and suggest you do this together for accountability.

LOVE YOURSELF FIRST

Many people regard singlehood as something they just need to survive until their next relationship and believe that, once in one, the pain of loneliness will end. But being single is a rich opportunity for inner growth and self-awareness that will undoubtedly improve the strength of the next relationship as well as decrease loneliness. Entering a new relationship often brings about some of life's greatest moments of joy. It also presents a whole new set of challenging feelings and can be our greatest mirror, reflecting the parts of ourselves we'd rather not face. When you are comfortable with who you are and your own company, you will be prepared for a relationship that challenges yet truly serves you.

A personality trait that can often cause strife in (and out) of relationships is perfectionism. As discussed in chapter 3, it is an unrealistic standard of expectations that leads to consistent disappointment, whether the expectation is achieved or not. A perfectionist will seek out the smallest of failures in order to continue the wild goose chase for something outside of themselves to fix in order to feel validated or accomplished. In a relationship, the significant other will, in time, begin to disappoint the perfectionist partner (or compete if they are one, too) and will either struggle endlessly to "make" their partner happy or eventually leave the relationship. One way to decrease perfectionism is to take stock of the "shoulds" you believe you must live by. For example, if you live close to your elderly parents, you may tell yourself, "I should be visiting them weekly or else I am a bad daughter/son," or "I should be able to endure my loneliness and not need any help." Consider where these beliefs originated and whether they are valid and worth the pain, guilt, or shame they are causing. Recognizing and healing perfection-istic tendencies is imperative to loving oneself.

CONCLUSION

I hope that this chapter enlightened you as to how important your relationship is with your-self, and showed you the benefits of solitude. In order to enjoy and connect with your true self, separating from self-critical thoughts and perfectionism will allow you to remain in the present. Additionally, creating more space for nurturing activities alone will provide your mind and body a welcome break in which to relax, restore, and open yourself to new experiences and greater moments of joy.

AFFIRMATIONS

I believe in the value of solitude.

I am able to take space for myself
when needed.

I know, at the core, I am good.

I am creating space in my life to connect
with my intuition.

I am committed to honoring myself
and practicing gratitude.

> *What's the greater risk? Letting go of what people think—or letting go of how I feel, what I believe, and who I am?*
> —BRENÉ BROWN

> *I am lonely, yet not everybody will do. I don't know why some people fill the gaps and others emphasize my loneliness.*
> —ANAÏS NIN

CHAPTER 5

The Foundation of a Healthy Relationship

Our relationships are the crux of who we are. Struggling under the weight of an unfulfilling or toxic one can wreak havoc on a person's self-esteem and outlook on life. Making the decision to break up, being broken up with, or attempting to heal a relationship can trigger a host of emotions. It may cause you to wonder if you are too demanding or whether you can ever find long-term happiness in an intimate relationship. Understanding what makes up the foundation of a healthy relationship, intimate or otherwise, will empower you to improve your current relationships and seek out new ones in an intentional way. This will involve clarifying your boundaries and assessing where adjustments may need to be made. Just as each person's wants and needs are unique, so too are their boundaries.

What may be important for one person—for example, freedom and autonomy—may be far less important for another who desires consistent connection and quality time. Yet each one is valid and deserves to be respected. Defining boundaries outside of intimate relationships also helps improve and preserve our connections with others, yet can often feel more challenging to express. This chapter will provide you with support in navigating the current landscape of dating, how to avoid the societal pressures around being single, and how to honor and trust in your own life's journey.

ESTABLISH BOUNDARIES

Whether the concept of boundaries is new to you or you feel that your boundaries are solidly in place, the work you have done in the preceding chapters may have given you a deeper understanding of your needs and expectations. The ability to respect your boundaries correlates to the level of authenticity in your connection with others, as well as yourself. When boundaries are out of balance and become either too rigid or too loose, your well-being pays the price. Inflexible boundaries trigger loneliness by preventing someone from trying new things out of their comfort zone or compromising with those around them. Alternatively, loose boundaries can attract a lot of friends, yet the relationships are shallow, reactive, or one-sided. A lack of boundaries becomes particularly evident during challenging times, as not having them decreases a person's ability to withstand the demands of others and zaps their energy.

During our childhood, we learned to manage our boundaries in whatever way we could to preserve a positive relationship with our caregivers. For example, if one of your parents struggled with anxiety or depression, you may have had to ignore your needs for autonomy in order to emotionally support your parent. In our adult relationships, we may unconsciously manage our boundaries the same way we did as children, by undermining or overriding our boundaries while telling ourselves our needs are excessive or invalid. Sometimes we hang on to the hope that the other person will magically change in the way we desire, perhaps the way we wished our caregivers would when we were children. As children we were limited in our ability to influence change, but as adults we must recognize our power. All too often we surrender and take the perspective of "it's just the way things are," or "no one else is happy in their relationship, why should I be?" We tolerate mistreatment or criticism masked as sarcasm, yet these things gradually break down our self-worth.

Our need for boundaries typically becomes strongest during our teenage years. Possessing verbal skills as well as an influx of hormones and a proclivity for risk-taking makes it easier to assert yourself. As we began to construct our identity, we craved autonomy, yet coveted peer connections and romantic interests. What was the general response from those around you as you began to stretch your wings and set boundaries? Do you feel that you were more or less able to navigate that period of your life following your own inner guide, or were you swept up in the expectations or perceptions of others? If your boundaries were consistently ignored, you may have begun to see your needs as inconsequential and an infringement upon others. You may have become overly involved in your friends' or family's lives, focusing on alleviating their problems or needs versus your own. As a result, not only do you allow others to ignore your boundaries, but you may violate them as well. This self-betrayal leads to a greater disconnect from your feelings and intuition. In order to find out what it is you truly want and need, you will have to distance yourself from the multiple layers of outside influence that have blocked you from hearing your intuition. Establishing boundaries will help you do just that.

Your needs will never cease to exist. Every day they are being met, consciously or unconsciously, in healthy or unhealthy ways. Think about a time when you felt undeserving of a certain need, yet still found a way to get it met. Often, people turn to manipulative measures in order to avoid directness and vulnerability. You may resort to giving insincere compliments, doing a multitude of favors, using guilt trips or even threats to ultimately get what you want. You may also identify yourself as a self-sacrificer, people pleaser, or victim, often making statements like "I do everything for others and never get anything in return," or "I can't say no," or "No one ever thinks about me." Where your needs begin and others' needs end is undefined. Clinically, these types of boundaries are termed as enmeshed, representing a lack of clear boundaries between two people that is problematic. In order to create defined boundaries, a shift must be made by focusing less on others' problems and more on your own. However, if you believe that being selfless is the only route to receiving love, avoiding your own needs may feel fundamental to experiencing connection. I often hear from clients the fear that if they do express their needs, and the other person is unable or unwilling to meet them, an irreversible rupture will occur, leading to permanent damage and potential abandonment. In order to create healthy boundaries, you must let go of the story that your needs do not matter or can only be validated by someone other than yourself.

When your boundaries are healthy, you feel grounded knowing that your words and actions are aligned with your values. You may feel some guilt in enforcing them, but it does not turn into shame because you are honoring your true self. You no longer need to rely on passive-aggressive tactics in order to get your needs met, or feel drained by the desire to fix other people's lives. Your life will become less chaotic and drama-filled. In order to make this change a reality, you must address the fear-based narratives in your mind. If not, these stories will continue to pull you into the same patterns again and again.

HONOR YOUR BOUNDARIES

As you begin to recognize where boundary changes need to be made, you will most likely stumble, either while implementing or following through on them. In the initial phase of any significant change, it is common to go back and forth on whether you should listen to your intuition. For my client Megan, her lack of boundaries with her parents became a significant part of our work together. She sought out therapy because she was struggling with questioning her career path. After eight years of education, she finally began her career as a dentist and hated it. She was battling intense critical thoughts around how she had chosen the wrong field, yet couldn't possibly change after so much time, money, and effort had been spent on the degree (in addition to the fact that her father was a dentist and found it a very rewarding career). As Megan began using the tools that would enable her to reconnect with her intuition, she realized how her parents' expectations for her had overruled her own interests and had dictated most of her life choices. She loved her parents dearly and knew they wanted the best for her, but she gradually recognized how far from her own path she had strayed in order to please them. This awareness allowed her to be more compassionate with herself as she eventually made the decision to change careers as well as to improve the boundaries between her and her parents.

There are many external triggers that can cause you to neglect your boundaries. If you are clear on your intention, you will be better prepared to overcome pressure that may feel overwhelming in the moment. Honoring your boundaries will also make more evident the situations where you tend to be manipulated or your needs regularly go ignored. Typically, people will respond to "boundary attacks" in one of three ways: aggressively, passively, or passive-aggressively. If responding aggressively, they may lash out when someone critiques them or crosses the line. This may work in training others not to cross a boundary, but they do so out of fear, not respect or understanding. Passive responses are also flawed in that they often require repeated enforcement. A passive person may be quick to apologize or say nothing at all in order to avoid conflict. But refusing to confront the issue does not mean the issue does not exist. Lastly, in passive-aggressive responses, a person does both. This response can often be unconscious, for example, a person makes an apology but later does something to hurt the other in retaliation. Instead of feeling vindicated, it actually makes them feel worse when they lash out at the other person in defense and out of the pain of the initial boundary-crossing.

As unhealthy as these patterns may seem, they can be very difficult to break, even with the best of intentions. What's important is to become more direct and assertive with your responses. Allow yourself to consider where the other person may be coming from or take time to clear up where there may have been a misunderstanding, but do not waffle on your boundaries, apologize for them, or ignore the fact that they have been crossed. Again, I know this can be quite challenging. Be compassionate with yourself and patient in this process. If a person truly cares about you, in time, they will come to understand how important your boundaries are to you and the relationship.

Get Comfortable with Saying No

Do you often say yes to things purely to avoid conflict, telling yourself that it is just easier that way and you'd rather not upset the other person? Or do you struggle with identifying how you truly feel in the moment, but feel pressured to make a decision, so you just go with whatever the other person wants?

A good first step toward recognizing your authentic response is to track your feelings after you agree to something. Anger, dread, or resentment are all signs that indicate the decision was not aligned with your wants or needs. Allowing your discomfort around saying no to overrule your needs often leads to power struggles, excuses, flakiness, or withdrawal, and eventual guilt. Taking the "easier" route does not come without consequences.

One way to shift course is to change your automatic reply from "Yes" to "Let me get back to you," or "I need to think about it." Doing so allows you to assess your feelings about what is being asked of you and to consider your schedule, energy level, and interest. If there is still a strong resistance to saying no, consider what may be influencing this. Is it fear of retaliatory anger or disappointment from the other person? It is possible that they will push back and try to convince you to change your mind. Remind yourself in these situations that they are allowed to have their feelings and, most importantly, so are you!

SOCIAL MEDIA MEDIATION

Another area of your life that may benefit from a boundary assessment is your social media use. Technology has made it nearly impossible not to be connected to someone or something (news, work, gaming), and can become obsessive without balanced boundaries. Excessive use of social media consumes your time by focusing on your virtual relationships versus in-real-life (IRL) ones, leading to an inferior sense of connection. Additionally, it can suck you into a comparison trap not based in reality, leading to fears of missing out (FOMO) and greater self-judgment. Technology can also dismantle socially appropriate interactions. For instance, asking someone to help you with your move or for a significant financial loan via text may feel much easier and less emotionally charged than asking face-to-face. In a television interview, singer-songwriter Ed Sheeran shared that he did not own a smartphone to avoid being inundated with requests: "I don't wake up in the morning and have to answer 50 messages of people asking for stuff." His experience is not solely one of a celebrity. My clients as well as friends will often lament their boss's lack of boundaries around texting at all hours of the morning, night, and weekend. Getting rid of your phone will, most likely, not be a possibility for you. Instead, try to challenge yourself with regulating your screen time. Following are a few tips to help you establish some social media boundaries:

- Set a time limit. Determine what you feel is a reasonable amount to spend on social media each day. This can be in one sitting or a total throughout the day.
- Make it a rule not to check social media when you are with others. Make the people in real life the priority, especially when they are right in front of you.
- Remove apps from either your phone or computer, or both. Do it as an experiment for a day, week, or month, or gradually start by removing them from your phone—usually the easiest way to check social media.

- Shift your mind-set. Remind yourself that the posts you see of someone's perfect vacation or family dinner are not a full representation. Consider whether checking a certain person's page will make you feel better or worse.
- Create a social media challenge with a friend. Changing patterns of behavior can often be easier when we make it a game or competition with a supportive friend.

BOUNDARY SETTING
FILL-IN-THE-BLANK

Consider a recent time when it was clear to you that your boundaries were being ignored, or that you would need to put some in place. With this experience in mind, complete the following sentences.

- A clear example of when my boundaries were ignored was

_____

_____

_____

- I did not feel comfortable speaking up for myself because

_____

_____

_____

- I tried to speak up for my needs and

_____

_____

_____

- My internal dialogue during or after sounded like

_____

_____

_____

- To feel more aligned with my feelings and needs, I will

_____

_____

_____

and

_____

_____

_____

Here are some prompts to use when setting a boundary:

- I would prefer not to . . .
- I have decided not to . . .
- I'll think about it.
- I feel uncomfortable . . .
- This is hard for me to say . . .
- I do mind that . . .
- I understand your point of view, but . . .

DETERMINE YOUR WANTS AND NEEDS IN INTIMATE RELATIONSHIPS

To go consciously into your next relationship, becoming clear on things you want and need will guide you toward the right partner for you. A "want" may be a partner who lives in the same neighborhood, has the same hobbies, or is in a certain profession. A "need" may be someone who is a good listener, enjoys spending time on their own, and isn't looking to get into a serious relationship too quickly. Homing in on a few of these wants and needs will help relieve some of the pressure of finding a "perfect" match and will make the dating process more enjoyable. When talking with my friend, Lily, she shared how being single at 38 has shifted her perspective on the type of love she is looking for.

"In my early 20s, it was all about infatuation and comfort, like puppy love. During my late 20s and early 30s, I wanted to find the kind of guy my parents and peers would approve of, a responsible guy who would also meet my need for validation and support. Now, my priorities have shifted. After being single for several years and seeing my friends go from one relationship to the next, fearing being alone for more than a couple of weeks, I've realized what is missing for them. Instead of

taking time to realize what makes them happy or what they truly want, they dive into the next relationship. In order to get validation from their partners, they end up compromising themselves to make it work. They focus more on presenting the ideal version of their relationship on Facebook versus the reality of how they feel in their day-to-day life. Eventually, it's just like they are coexisting, both afraid to end it. I believe that because of my years of being single as a full-fledged adult, I have learned I do not need to seek or earn validation from my partner. I am happy with myself and don't beat myself up as much as I did in my 20s. I know that improving my self-esteem is my job. What I'm hoping for in my next relationship is a mature love; one in which there isn't pressure on either one of us to be that person's entire life, but instead to complement each other's existing lives and make them even better."

As we age, we become more cognizant of the lessons of past relationships, and observing those around us allows us to create our own unique formula for compatibility—for example, similar temperaments, goals, and values. Possessing a solid sense of self allows one to gain clarity on the traits that will lead to long-term sustainability as a couple, as well as to discern what traits are truly important to us versus the ones that are important to our family, friends, and peers.

RELATIONSHIP INVENTORY

In your journal, write an inventory of your past intimate relationships. Think about how clear you were regarding your wants and needs with each partner.

1. Before your last relationship, did you have certain traits in mind that you wanted your next partner to possess?
2. Did they end up having those traits, or were they quite different from what you were looking for?
3. What made you ignore those differences?
4. Were they traits that you came around to appreciating, or were they ignored in hopes of change?
5. Was it harder or easier to communicate your sexual needs versus emotional needs?
6. If your ability to share varied greatly, depending on the partner, what traits do you think were necessary to support you in voicing them?
7. Using this information, create a list of wants and needs for your future or current relationship.

COMMUNICATE CLEARLY

When we can effectively communicate our needs and boundaries with someone, we build a connection based on authenticity and respect. Unfortunately, we often become distracted by the chatter in our mind, instructing us what to say in order to impress or appear good enough. Yet by challenging the chatter and allowing ourselves to be vulnerable, we create the possibility for our needs to be met while enhancing the quality of the relationship. Still, we resist doing so, usually out of fear of being seen as too needy or sensitive. We also fall prey to the belief that those closest to us can read our minds, expecting that they possess the magical ability to always know what we are thinking and feeling without having to tell them. As convenient as that would be, it is unrealistic and creates even greater feelings of disconnection. Additionally, when emotions have been bottled up, it can be quite difficult to calmly articulate thoughts and feelings while remaining attuned to the other person. The weight of the pain and hurt we have kept inside can override our ability to consider their experience or point of view and can further sideline the opportunity for resolution or understanding.

Often our family's ability to express emotions impacts how we communicate our feelings with others. Many learn early on that talking about feelings makes others uncomfortable. We are taught that negative feelings should be brushed under the rug so that we will not be seen as weak or a complainer. Yet left unsaid, the hurt remains and manifests itself in a lack of trust. Over time, withdrawal often manifests into indifference; the opposite of love or connection. Buried feelings also carry over into other relationships, especially intimate ones. At the start of a romantic relationship, a significant part of our attraction stems from how seen and understood we feel. As time progresses, conflicts will inevitably arise but go unaddressed in hopes of preserving the initial connection. But ignoring feelings like frustration, disappointment, and anger prevents deeper intimacy. Following an argument, it is natural to experience some distance between you and your partner, a "cooldown" period. Understanding this as a normal part of resolving differences will help decrease anxiety that may arise around losing the other person, which often inhibits one from sharing their authentic feelings.

Dr. John Gottman , a prominent relationship researcher, has spent decades studying the ways in which couples handle conflict, claiming a 90 percent predictability rate of identifying the relationships that will last. Some of the red flags signaling a breakdown in connection include name-calling, attacking their partner's character, inability to take in feedback, and avoiding confrontations. Ultimately, he found the most significant indicator of long-term relationship sustainability is the way in which a couple fights and how they move on from it.

The strongest test for self-awareness is how we handle intimate relationships. The way in which you respond to conflict with your significant other (as well as friends and family) can highlight areas in need of attention or compassion, as well as possible boundary setting. For example, Andrew, a client of mine, noticed that his recent fights with his partner would swiftly accelerate to the point where he felt like he would explode and yell very hurtful things at his partner. I encouraged him to develop a plan with his partner to recognize when they needed a break before an argument escalated to a level at which he no longer felt in control. They agreed to take their dog for a walk or go to separate rooms for at least thirty minutes. Doing this allowed Andrew to process his and his partner's feelings without having to respond immediately, usually out of defensiveness. When they resumed their discussion, he was able to more accurately communicate his needs and feelings.

It is very common to feel vulnerable during an argument, and our instinct is to either defend or attack in order to avoid criticism or judgment. This mode of responding may help you regain a sense of control or power in the moment, but it does little to address the underlying needs, leading to the same fights over and over again.

As you work on improving your relationships, it is important to remember that your partner is on their own path and comes with their own history and experiences. Expectations for the one perfect partner to rescue you will inevitably fall short, especially as conflict surfaces. Understanding that marriage requires constant care will enable you to be more patient and compassionate throughout your entire journey together, not just during the good parts. Seeing your significant other as an imperfect companion on your life's journey, not as someone to complete you or as your savior, will allow for the harmony you seek.

LOVE LANGUAGES—HOW TO UNDERSTAND YOUR PARTNER'S AND YOUR NEEDS WITH EASE

A very popular book that addresses the varying ways we give and receive love is Gary Chapman's *The Five Love Languages*. Chapman, a counselor, realized how important it was for couples to understand that their way of receiving love may be quite different from their partner's. For example, if quality time is a person's love language, they will appreciate their spouse scheduling an intimate evening more than they will appreciate receiving the perfect gift. Even though each of the five languages is beneficial to a happy and healthy relationship, there is typically one that is most important to each person. When this love language is consistently employed, the quality of the relationship and connection improves significantly. The five languages are:

1. Words of affirmation: genuine terms of endearment, encouragement, appreciation, and assurance
2. Quality time: focused, uninterrupted time together engaged in meaningful connection
3. Receiving gifts: simple, sentimental objects or thoughtful gifts they know their partner will appreciate

4. **Acts of service: planning and effort is put forth to support their partner or ease their burden in some way**
5. **Physical touch: small touches throughout the day or frequent hugs provide a sense of connection and security**

DETERMINING YOUR LOVE LANGUAGE

After reading about the different forms of showing and receiving love, were you able to identify your own love language? Whether you were able to determine yours easily or felt torn between two or three, write out your responses to the following questions to clarify why receiving love in that way is important to you. If you'd like to learn more or take a quiz in order to determine your love language, you can visit the website at www.5lovelanguages.com.

- What do you think your love language is and why?
- What emotional need(s) was not being met in past relationships?
- What love languages do you feel comfortable expressing to your partner and which ones, if any, do you struggle with? What makes them uncomfortable for you?

RESIST THE PRESSURE

In spite of the fact that the divorce rate of the United States is the third highest in the world, with nearly half of all marriages ending in divorce, there still exists a strong societal pressure to get married. The terrain of relationships has shifted significantly; there is more freedom to date whomever you like and to marry later, yet the stigma around being single remains. Why is this the case? What makes singlehood so difficult for others to accept?

Those who naysay singlehood tend to do so out of fear for a variety of reasons. For instance, they may have struggled with deep loneliness while single and are concerned that you will have the same experience. One of the most damaging beliefs is that a single person's life has little purpose or meaning. Often their successes and achievements are glossed over because they do not have a partner and are still seen as "failing" in the relationship department. Understandably, many people succumb to the pressure and enter into relationships while ignoring red flags. Or they force themselves to date when they are not ready, which can lead to even greater pain and frustration. Even though the external expectations of others have been met, the internal battle worsens. When they are on the wrong path, their intuition will confront them in whatever way it can, over time growing louder and louder. Subscribing to this fear-based perspective takes them out of the richness of the present and keeps them focused on either the potential of the future or woes of the past.

Alternatively, when you let go of the belief that you can only be happy while in a relationship, you open yourself up to the unique opportunity that being single provides. Not only do you have more time to do what you want, when you want, but you establish a trust and faith within yourself that will carry you through whatever hardships you might face. When you do choose to start dating or enter a relationship, you can do so freely and not out of fear.

CONCLUSION

Through the reading and self-reflection exercises in this chapter, you should feel more confident expressing your needs and how to go about communicating them in a more direct and clear way. You may have recognized the ways in which you violate your own boundaries and are considering steps to take in order to honor your needs, feelings, and unique life path. Additionally, you may have realized where you need to create or redraw boundaries with certain people in order to foster a more respectful and connected relationship. In chapter 6, we'll delve into the steps you can take to expand your social circle and improve your current relationships.

AFFIRMATIONS

I believe that drawing boundaries is important.

I communicate my wants and needs clearly.

I let go of what other people think.

I am constantly developing and growing in my relationships.

I deserve to have healthy relationships.

Emptiness which is conceptually liable to be mistaken for sheer nothingness is in fact the reservoir of infinite possibilities.
—D. T. SUZUKI

I am lonely, sometimes, but I dare say it's good for me.
—LOUISA MAY ALCOTT, *LITTLE WOMEN*

CHAPTER 6

Connect with Confidence

I have no doubt that you've had numerous talks with yourself or been told by others to just get out there and meet new people, especially after a breakup. I know how frustrating it can be to attend an event and return home not having spoken to a single person. Or worse, going on date after date with little or no spark, feeling agitated and wishing you just stayed home instead. Yet no matter how many bad dates you go on, your desire for connection will never go away. This chapter will help you change these experiences to feel less like a burden and instead make them more enjoyable and fulfilling. Connecting with confidence is a skill that only improves with practice. By stepping out of your comfort zone and embracing vulnerability, you become more approachable and attract the kind of relationships you want in your life. You will also trust yourself to let go of the relationships that no longer serve you in order to make room for the ones that will. When we are self-confident, we can more easily ignore the critical thoughts that put us in our own way and care less about what other people might think about us. We can create major shifts in our lives when we believe in ourselves and our worth.

TRY SOMETHING NEW

Stepping out of our comfort zone is not easy. The explanation is in the name; we are comfortable where we are, not because it actually makes us happy, but it's what we know, and the known is easier to handle than the unknown. We think that by avoiding change, we will feel more secure. The truth is that focusing on maintaining the status quo keeps you in a fearful and insecure state of mind. If we choose to live our lives within the confines of a safe zone, there exists little opportunity for the rewards that come with vulnerability. New experiences help challenge our brains, foster healthier habits, and decrease loneliness. Yet knowing something could be good for you and doing it are two different beasts. In order to act, we need to truly believe in the value of doing so, especially if it is an affront to the status quo. When we are focused only on the next day, week, or month, doing something that comes with a longer-term payoff is harder to invest our time and effort in. The critic's voice will happily point out all of the things that are either more important (usually something that may involve a commitment to someone else) or less risky in order to avoid potential failure.

In order to get out of your own way, take a step back from looking at what is right in front of you and get a more long-term perspective on your life. Doing so allows you to recognize the unnecessary tasks, distractions, and excuses that all add up to time lost and goals unmet. For example, can you recall a time in your life when, after enjoying something you'd wanted to do for a while, you thought, "Why didn't I do this sooner?" My client Zoe was facing rebuilding her life after her nine-year relationship ended. After she moved out of the apartment they shared and began to feel more settled, she was confronted with the fact that her non-work time had been mostly consumed by her ex and his interests. She realized how little she enjoyed the activities they used to do together, but felt lost as to what she would like to do, especially on her own. We talked through interests she had prior to the relationship and what could potentially feel challenging, fun, or fulfilling. She recalled feeling inspired by a Spanish language class she took in college and had always dreamt of traveling to Spain, but her partner preferred to only travel within the United States. She decided to enroll in a free language course offered by the local community college and at the end of the year booked a solo trip. She couldn't believe she was acting on this dream and afterward wished she hadn't waited so long. She continued taking classes to improve her Spanish skills and connected with a few people from class who have since become close friends.

There may be a variety of reasons not to incorporate new activities into your life. You may feel overwhelmed by your current responsibilities and commitments, and fitting something else in just feels like too much. Taking time away from work and financial demands can feel like a hindrance. For many, life is about being productive; earning and saving money is the highest priority or value. Spending money on things that do not fall into these categories, like an art class or a ticket to a symphony, may feel like a lavish expense or frivolous. Yet no matter where you live, there are most likely options for free or inexpensive activities, such as community yoga classes, performances in a park, or a free day at a museum. Volunteering is also a way to explore your interests while helping a cause. Alternatively, you may have a lot of time that could be spent doing something new, but the question remains, what? Or you have attempted new hobbies, but nothing seems to stick.

For people who struggle with perfectionism, trying something new can be especially challenging. To attempt something new generally means you are at a beginner's level. Proficiency will take time and dedicated practice. If you don't have the confidence to be okay with failing or aren't motivated enough to commit the time, the new hobby can easily lose its luster. Whatever your reason is for not incorporating new activities into your life, I ask that you remain open to the possibility as you continue through this book and consider where small changes can be made.

THE BENEFIT OF KEEPING A SOCIAL SCHEDULE

Prioritizing and creating a social schedule is a great tool for decreasing loneliness. Just as you may keep a calendar for work tasks or life responsibilities, a social schedule will keep the need for connection on your mind as you determine your priorities for the day, week, or month ahead. You may find that you feel like everyone has plans or is booked—that's because they have prioritized their social schedule and made commitments in order to address their needs and invest in their connection with others. Just like with other things that have become routine or a habit, it is useful to change your mind-set to *"I need to have plans made for X number of nights a week"* or *"I need to reach out to X people by Wednesday of each week."*

Traveling Solo

Traveling is great for the soul. It takes you out of your routine and allows you to be truly present in the moment. When you travel, it is like seeing things again with childlike wonder. You are exposed to different ways of life, the uniqueness that each town, city, or country possesses. Especially when you may be feeling bored, agitated, or depressed, changing your environment can help you heal or have a different perspective. Traveling alone can also give you the freedom to remove the mask you may wear around co-workers or loved ones. You can be in your sadness without having to apologize for or hide from it. Traveling solo doesn't require you to be entirely by yourself; joining a travel group or signing up for a retreat can be a great way to connect with new people. Although I am a big believer in the value of staycations, especially when travel is not possible due to financial or other constraints, immersing yourself in a new environment forces you to be without the comforts of home and provides the opportunity to feel most at home in yourself. One caveat is that as beneficial as traveling or even moving to a new city may be, it does not provide an automatic reset to your life. As Jon Kabat-Zinn explores in his best-selling book, *Wherever*

You Go, There You Are: Mindfulness Meditation in Everyday Life, your thoughts follow you no matter where you are and will eventually catch up with you, regardless of distractions or a new environment.

Traveling is another tool for gaining a different and more positive perspective, potentially paving the way to healing the relationship with yourself. Additional benefits to traveling solo include:

- The necessity to ask for help (e.g., asking for directions) forces you to talk to strangers and potentially strike up a conversation and connection.
- Asking for help also exposes you to the kindness of strangers and may inspire you to pass on the good deed to someone else.
- You can connect with others over shared experiences and hear their unique stories and backgrounds.
- Sharing new experiences with others creates powerful bonds.
- Traveling gives you a chance to take a break from people in your life who bring you down and zap your energy.
- You can be a new person, free to speak, dress, and even eat in different ways.
- Trying new things improves our resiliency and self-confidence.

CONVERSATION STARTERS

It can be enormously helpful to have some tried-and-true ways to start a conversation in your back pocket whenever you go somewhere with the opportunity to make new connections. Here are some ideas to get you started, but I encourage you to create your own list of at least five behaviors that would help you feel comfortable initiating a dialogue.

- Pay the person a compliment. Try to notice something unique about them that can be fodder for easy conversation.
- Be self-admonishing and ask for help. It can be as simple as asking where the restroom is or what their opinion is on a menu item.
- If you are not an avid news watcher, take a glance at Google News or subscribe to newsletters like theSkimm that offer snippets of world affairs with some humor added in. This also includes pop culture, an easy and perhaps less-charged way to engage with others.
- Know a few jokes that you are great at delivering and can lighten the mood.
- Stick to asking open-ended questions—questions that do not have a yes or no response.
- Pose a question that is tailored for a group setting; for example, what would everyone's favorite day consist of or who are three people they admire and why?

CONTINUED >>

CONTINUED >>

- Offer to help them! If you see someone is struggling with their map, ask them if they need directions, or hold the door open for someone who has their hands full.
- Show your vulnerability. Admit that you are nervous or don't know anyone—it can instantly help the other person feel less alone.

Take Small Steps

Trying something new can be daunting in many ways. It's best to plan out small steps in the direction of your goal with a lot of self-compassion and positive reinforcement along the way. For example, if your goal is to speak to strangers with greater ease, you can challenge yourself to ask the cashier at the checkout counter how they are doing and truly pause to hear their answer. A friend recently shared with me how she feels so welcomed by the people at her bank that she will respond to their question "How are you?" with an honest answer, even if she isn't having a good day. She appreciates their kindness and sees these encounters as a minimally stressful way of engaging authentically with strangers. These might seem like insignificant connections, but they will build on each other over time and help relieve feelings of loneliness.

It can also be helpful to start by objectively tracking yourself throughout your day and noticing the ways in which you engage with a colleague, family member, or friend:

- Where are the opportunities for connection that you dismiss or shy away from and why?
- What is your body language when you engage? Are your arms open or crossed? Are you smiling? Are you sitting at your desk, still facing your computer?
- Do you show an interest in their life or in areas of common ground?
- In what ways can you let people in more?

Having pictures on your desk of your pet, family, or other interests can be a great conversation opener. You can challenge yourself to make eye contact and smile at every person that passes. If it's a particularly rough day, a conversation may just be held with children or pets.

When you set goals for yourself, it is helpful to phrase the goal in a positive way, similar to affirmations. Doing so helps trick and reset the brain to think more confidently. Instead of thoughts like "I'm going to try or attempt to reach this goal," shift them to something like "I will have no problem making this goal" or "I know I am going to be successful." This will help your actions become more aligned with your thoughts in the way you want. I recommend naming this optimistic voice after a person like a loving grandparent, cool aunt, or simply a cheerleader who always believes the best of you. It allows you to pivot your thoughts more easily into the direction you desire.

ACTIVITY PLAN

You may feel stuck on what steps you should take to strengthen or build new connections. When we slow down and allow ourselves to become quiet, we can better connect with the part of ourselves that knows the next steps to take. Yet we often resist what we want to do and may return to it several times before finally following through. This is the challenge and moment of opportunity for change. Journal about how you are currently filling your time.

- If it's helpful, grab your day planner and get clear on where your time is being spent.
- Do you allow yourself time and space to meet or engage with others for fun?
- If so, where can you increase that time or change it up in some way?
- If not, make a list of at least 10 things that you have an interest in that involve other people and choose one to pursue for the following week.

BUILDING EMPATHY FOR OTHERS

We can more easily connect with others when we empathize with their point of view. Empathy means putting yourself in another person's shoes in order to more clearly understand their feelings. However, we do not take on their situation or problem as our own. We become curious, nonjudgmental, and observe without attaching to a certain outcome. This allows for improved listening and less advice giving, which can shut down authentic connection. Stephen Covey, author of *The 7 Habits of Highly Effective People,* said, "Seek first to understand, then to be understood." Learning how to empathize with others is an incredibly useful skill and can be applied in many areas of your life.

Some things to keep in mind when practicing empathy:

- Try to feel grounded within yourself; take deep breaths, set an intention, become more mindful of the moment and the other person.
- Mirror the other person's emotions and body language. If they are excited, show your excitement; if they are sad, be there with them. Don't feel you need to fix or change their feelings.
- Keep eye contact steady, but with breaks.
- Do not disregard the other person's feelings or reasons for their feelings. Do not excuse, defend, or make light of them.

- Take time to ask thoughtful questions that will help you understand their situation better.
- Don't change the topic to your experience right away or relate theirs to someone you know or what you read or saw on TV.
- Preface any suggestions as just that—suggestions that they may ignore or might consider trying; it's totally up to them.
- If connecting over email or text, try to match the length of responses. If they are writing paragraphs, try to do the same versus one-word or emoticon responses.

THE POWER OF YOUR BODY LANGUAGE

There are many nonverbal cues you give to those around you that signal your openness. You may be one of the kindest souls on the planet, but many people miss out because your eyes are always looking down or your arms are crossed. Not only does your body language communicate to others, but it also impacts how you feel about yourself. Track the way you carry yourself throughout the day:

- Do you stand tall, with shoulders back and head held high?
- Do you sit with legs and arms crossed off to the side?
- Try different poses and see if doing so shifts your mood or garners a different response from the people around you.

By and large, the more space you take up translates to confidence and approachability. A great TED talk with over 50 million views is Amy Cuddy's, titled "Your Body Language Shapes Who You Are." She shares her research on how standing or sitting in certain postures can improve your feelings of confidence and contribute to greater success in your life.

START WITH YOUR COMMUNITY

As you take steps to build your connections, a great way to start is to lean on the people who are already in your life. Whether that's family, friends, colleagues, or the community where you live, don't be afraid to strengthen those connections and ask for help widening your circle of friends (just make sure that you aren't depending on people who have let you down in the past). Family gatherings, housewarming parties, and double dates are all great ways to meet new people in a low-pressure way. I think it is also worth noting how worthwhile it is to give a second chance to a family member who you may have had conflict with in the past. If your only way of contact is at important family events, you may not be aware of their own inner growth. Just as you are taking steps to change the way you interact with others, take note of changes in the people around you as well.

Another way for you to expand your social circle is to challenge yourself to say yes to every invitation that comes your way if it is in alignment with your newfound sense of self and how you are comfortable connecting with the world. When we get into the habit of turning down invitations or canceling at the last minute, we're seen as unreliable and are less likely to be invited to things in the future. In Shonda Rhimes's book, *The Year of Yes*, she shares how a lovingly simple confrontation with her sister regarding the fact that she rarely said yes to things spurred her to dedicate a year of her life to doing just that. In spite of being an introvert and having intense fears of large social gatherings, she writes about how saying yes transformed her life in ways she never imagined.

Your ability to feel part of a community begins with the capacity to be your most authentic self. When you feel that you truly belong, you no longer get distracted or overwhelmed by seeking approval or wanting to fit in. You are able to be a part of something, yet also stand alone.

WHY FACE-TO-FACE IS BEST

Even though technology has become the easiest way to engage with others, meeting in person remains the best way to determine how well you will connect with someone. Using your phone, computer, or a dating app can be efficient and enable you to avoid potential awkward or uncomfortable encounters. However, a study done by Ohio State University found that online dating increases feelings of social anxiety and loneliness for people who identify with those feelings prior to signing onto the apps. This points to the fact that as our dependence on technology *increases*, our ability to confidently engage in person *decreases*. For those who already struggle with in-person interactions, solely focusing your efforts online will negatively impact your ability to engage with people in real life. As you become more used to a superficial way of engaging, your potential for deeper intimacy becomes further limited.

In order to ease the task of connecting with people face-to-face, it is helpful to adopt the perspective of curiosity. Start off a date with a question or intention of learning something unique about the other person or of finding a common thread between the two of you. There is always something! People like to be listened to with genuine interest. In this way, you can exchange your self-consciousness with care for the other person. This perspective can help you feel more grounded and calm and it provides a level of protection from the internal critic.

Developing connections takes time. Focusing your efforts on meeting someone in person versus online can be cumbersome, to say the least, especially since it makes it harder to avoid the unpleasantness of rejecting someone or of being rejected. But the true richness of life comes from exposing ourselves to a variety of people and experiences. When we believe in the value and potential magic of striking up a conversation with a stranger, our lives open up to greater possibilities inside and outside of romantic relationships.

Dating Mantras

I want to have integrity with myself and others and remain open, with compassion and curiosity.

I am ready to engage with new people with gratitude and open my heart to these experiences.

HOW TO MEET PEOPLE OFFLINE

One of the first things to do when you want to try to meet people offline is to determine your mind-set. Creating a mantra to remind you of your intention as you put yourself out there and allow yourself to be vulnerable is a true test of confidence. Any way that you can decrease the pressure on yourself will pay dividends when taking risks you wouldn't normally take. It is also immensely helpful to not take yourself too seriously. Making light of the situation can put you and the other person at ease. Another important reminder is to not judge a book by its cover. First impressions can often be wrong or offer just one side of a person. Remember that our mind is actively searching for things to help us rule out or avoid any form of danger. This blocks us from taking time to get to know someone better or from reaching out in a meaningful way. And, last but not least, remove your dating apps from your phone. This will help you stay off the apps in order to retrain your brain to meet people in real life.

KNOW WHEN YOU ARE READY TO DATE AGAIN (AND WHEN YOU'RE NOT!)

There is no one right length of time to wait to begin dating again after a breakup. There are a multitude of sayings and nuggets of advice about how to get over your ex and move on, but, ultimately, you will take action when it feels right for you. After reading this far and working through the exercises in this book, you should have more insight regarding what you do and do not want in your next relationship. Determining whether you are in a good state of mind to find a person who meets your expectations will help you avoid turning dating into a stressful and unenjoyable process. Dating is difficult for everyone, but an optimistic mind-set will make the experience more enjoyable and one in which you can feel relaxed and be yourself. If you are unsure whether or not you would like to start dating again, here are some things to consider:

- Do you feel excited when you consider meeting someone for a date?
- Do you believe there is an abundance of good, trustworthy people and you just have to find the right one for you?
- Is any part of your interest in dating to make your ex jealous?

- Are you hoping to find someone to fill a void?
- Are you still following your ex on social media or trying to connect in hopes of reuniting?
- Do you understand the reason you broke up with your ex and feel ready to apply what you learned to the next relationship?
- Do you feel okay with giving up some freedom and autonomy to be in a relationship?
- Are you feeling pessimistic, defeated, or cynical about ever finding someone again?

I understand how much pressure there is to be actively dating when you are single, but I hope that after reading about the positive impact solitude and self-reflection can have on your life, you are able to disregard others' expectations. If you feel that you would rather spend more time uncoupled, doing the things you enjoy, and getting to know yourself better, more power to you! It is not unusual once you have begun the journey of self-introspection to crave more. It is immensely freeing to feel grounded in your own self-worth, unencumbered by the influence of others. Possessing a deep trust in yourself allows you to do things that result in your own happiness and contentment, irrespective of the understanding or approval of others. Honor this part of your life and trust in the timing of your own journey. When you are ready to date, you will feel confident in your ability to stay true to yourself above all else.

CONCLUSION

My hope is that, after reading this chapter, you feel more prepared to take action to bring about the change you want in your life. Healing loneliness is truly about the quality of your connections, not the quantity. We can feel so confused when we struggle with loneliness, even though our lives may appear "normal" on the outside. Yet what we are searching for has become harder to find as our current modes of connecting create barriers to deep connection. By trying activities that engage the mind and body, like traveling, conversing with strangers, or meeting potential dates in real life versus online, your world and heart will begin to open up.

AFFIRMATIONS

I see the good in others and they see the
good in me.

I step out of my comfort zone in
order to grow.

I open my heart to relationships
that are supportive.

I grow my community with ease.

I am optimistic about my life
and my future.

What should young people do with their lives today? Many things, obviously. But the most daring thing is to create stable communities in which the terrible disease of loneliness can be cured.
–KURT VONNEGUT, *PALM SUNDAY: AN AUTOBIOGRAPHICAL COLLAGE*

You think your pain and your heartbreak are unprecedented in the history of the world, but then you read. It was [books] that taught me that the things that tormented me most were the very things that connected me with all the people who were alive, who had ever been alive.
—JAMES BALDWIN

CHAPTER 7

The Loneliness Solution

Congratulate yourself on making it to the final chapter of this book. Hopefully, by opening yourself up to support in this way, you have experienced some relief and feel even more empowered than when you started to continue healing your loneliness. The likelihood of lasting change improves with patience, vulnerability, and self-compassion. Give yourself time to process and reprocess what you have read, acknowledging even the smallest steps or mental shifts. Experiencing loneliness does not mean you are flawed or incapable of building healthy relationships. To be human is to feel lonely, enriching the moments when we do feel connected and happy. It is not a part of your identity, nor do you need to change who you are. Further, as a result of your experience of loneliness, you are even more attuned to genuine, authentic connection.

Given that the landscape of our society has shifted so rapidly in the way we connect, it is important to recognize these changes and learn how to adjust in order to maintain and create fulfilling connection. Due to the short- and long-term impact loneliness has on our physical, mental, and emotional well-being, it is imperative we do this for ourselves as well as for future generations. Using the practical tools in this book will help you see the blind spots that exist in your current relationships and provide you with a guide to create better relationships in the future. Above all, prioritizing the improvement of your self-esteem and believing in your self-worth will enable you to find peace in moments of solitude and give you clarity about your needs and the things that bring you happiness. This chapter will introduce a few more tools and highlight ways for you to continue combating loneliness on your own. These exercises and strategies can be used daily and can be revisited whenever you need reminders or supportive encouragement.

YOUR BODY IS YOUR HOME—TAKE CARE OF IT

Our mind and body function as a team, and caring for both is imperative to maintaining good health and well-being. As we age, it becomes more apparent what impacts our body in a positive or negative way. Making choices to maintain a strong body and mind requires discipline and a dedication to a lifestyle that prioritizes your health. Following are areas of focus for taking care of your body and mind.

Sleep: One of the greatest positive shifts I've seen in my clients comes about when they are able to improve their sleep. Whether it is the quality or quantity, when sleep is an issue, it can cause a great amount of anxiety and trigger other unhealthy behaviors. The cycle of restless nights followed by exhausted days impacts many areas of our lives, often invisible to those around us. Without nourishing sleep, the brain loses its ability to restore itself and it requires much more effort to think clearly or critically. Exhaustion leads to less self-control around food and more irritability. When it's chronic, a cloud of haziness and a struggle just to make it through the day can easily lead to isolation. If you relate to one or all of these symptoms, know that you are not alone. There are steps you can take to improve your sleep, and like most change, it will likely require some trial and error. Trust that challenging yourself to try the following suggestions can lead to a very positive impact on your quality of life.

- Stick to a regular bedtime.
- Stop screen time one hour before bed.
- Keep your phone charging in another room and put it on Do Not Disturb.
- Make the room as dark as possible.
- Use a sound machine, fan, or white noise.
- Make sure you are as comfortable as possible—use clean sheets, cozy pajamas, and aromatherapy.
- Breathe deeply or meditate.
- Journal your thoughts.
- Exercise before bed.

Movement: Along with the change in our society's way of communicating, the way we use our bodies throughout the day has also changed. For many, day-to-day physical movements include sitting in a car to and from work, sitting at a desk for several hours at a time, sitting at home to eat and watch TV, and then finally lying down to sleep. A sedentary lifestyle has been identified as a risk factor for cardiovascular disease Type 2 diabetes, obesity, anxiety, and depression. Just like sleep, integrating regular movement throughout your day in whatever way you can is imperative for a healthy mind and body. Following are a few ideas for adding movement to your day.

- **Stretching:** Giving your body a good stretch throughout the day is an excellent way to connect with the body and see where you may be holding some tension or tightness. You can do some light stretches almost anywhere and instantly feel more grounded and relaxed.
- **Yoga:** The benefits of yoga include greater flexibility, muscle strength, improved respiration, and energy. Options for yoga are endless; classes can be individual or group-style, indoors, outdoors, or online.
- **Walking:** Walking remains one of the best and easiest ways to move your body. Find ways to add more walking to your daily routine. For example, go for a walk during lunch or after dinner.
- **Dance:** Whether you are "good" at dancing or not, moving your body to your favorite music is

an easy and fun way to feel connected to your body. Listening to music you enjoy is a good motivator. Spend some time creating a playlist to enjoy and listen to as you start or end your day.

- **Meditation:** There are various forms of meditation; just a few of the most popular include Loving-kindness, body scan or progressive relaxation, mindfulness, breath awareness, Kundalini yoga, and Transcendental Meditation. I hope that the meditations in the earlier chapters felt supportive to you, especially if it was your first experience with meditation. I encourage you to research why meditation has been such a widely used tool for positive mental and physical health.

SPEND TIME IN NATURE

What is your relationship with nature? Do you seek it out for relaxation, adventure, or physical activity? Did you enjoy nature as a child? There are a multitude of benefits that come from spending time in nature. It engages our senses in a way that few other activities can. Extensive research shows that being in nature reduces

MOVEMENT PLAN

Grab your journal or calendar and create a movement plan for yourself. If you are someone who likes variety, challenge yourself to try an assortment of movement ideas to keep you inspired. Make your plan an attainable one; for example, stretch for three minutes in bed before going to sleep. You can make exercise progressively more active as you become more comfortable integrating it into your day as an enjoyable form of movement.

stress, improves memory, and decreases anxiety and depression. It can also have an immediate impact on your mood. Especially if you live in an urban area, it is important you make being out in nature a priority as you work toward decreasing your loneliness.

WALKING MEDITATION

A form of meditation that is very simple and accessible throughout your day is a walking meditation. Ideally, you can do this meditation out in nature and barefoot, but anywhere you have space to walk will work. Just find a quiet place that will allow for at least 15 paces. Start with your feet firmly planted on the ground and close your eyes.

- Take a deep breath in and out.
- Notice how it feels to be standing solidly in place. Notice any other senses from the top of your head down to your toes.
- Gently open your eyes and take in the surroundings.
- Start to walk very slowly, placing one foot gently yet firmly in front of the other.

- With each step, slowly pick your foot off the earth and then slowly drop it back to the earth.
- Once you have taken about 15 paces, stop and pause to close your eyes and take another deep breath.
- Turn around and return to your original spot.
- Just like in a sitting meditation, try not to let your mind wander to other things. Gently bring it back to your steps.
- You can adjust your speed as you like, going back and forth for ideally 20 minutes.

If you are able to do this meditation in nature, walking in the grass barefoot is a very effective way to change your mood. Either way, you will most likely feel relaxed and calm after your walking meditation.

BUILD A COMMUNITY AROUND YOU

A way to provide yourself with a solid foundation of support and connection is to build a community of people you enjoy spending time with, and who care about you. As discussed in chapter 1, technology and the fact that we are a very transient generation has led to a breakdown in community. People are much less likely to know their neighbors, local shopkeepers, etc. As a result of improvements in efficiency, the ways of connecting with those in our community have slowly diminished. There are so many online services now that offer delivery for anything you might need (e.g., food, laundry, groceries), that you rarely need to leave your home.

Additionally, as the workforce has begun to embrace and encourage working from home, the bonds created in the work environment have fallen away. There may be communication via email or conference calls, but little is shared around each other's personal lives. Working from home does provide a certain number of conveniences but can lead to isolation and a decrease in team morale. If you are someone who works from home, establishing regular coffee shops to visit and making a point of talking to the staff will help provide you with a community outside of the traditional office atmosphere. Additionally, there are coworking spaces that provide a form of connection among the other visitors or members.

A great way to build community is to choose a hobby you are interested in and commit to it. Take a class, offer to teach, or volunteer—whatever you can do that puts you in the same space with others who share your interests. With consistency, you are bound to create connections that will expand your community in ways you may have never imagined.

THE VALUE OF NOT DOING EVERYTHING YOURSELF

As much as we are taught that strength is exhibited by not needing anything from others, we may end up appearing strong, yet feel terrible inside because it feels like we carry the weight of the world on our shoulders. As a result, we often feel burned out and terrified of asking for help. The truth is, asking for help is one of the greatest signs of strength, and people feel a sense of inner value when they are able to help another person. But you may feel too vulnerable asking someone for support. In either scenario, as a culture, we need to do better at communicating what we need and let go of the belief that doing everything ourselves is best. Consider where in your life you feel overwhelmed and could ask for help, even just to talk it out with someone. Additionally, consider what tasks you could possibly delegate to others that would allow you to spend more time on the things you truly enjoy.

SELF-FULFILLING PROPHECY

Expectations can be a good or bad thing, depending on your mind-set. We may not want certain things to happen in our lives but for some reason come to expect them, and eventually they do take place. This doesn't mean that just because you think a bad thing might happen, it will. But your expectations do influence your actions, and your actions contribute to your life's narrative. Expectations are often triggered by a past experience that normalizes the next occurrence, so it is completely understandable why you may have them. But recognizing how they may be keeping you stuck will hopefully allow you to shift your expectations toward the possibility of change and be open to having more in your life.

Journal about the expectations you have around changing your loneliness or quality of connection with others.

- Does the possibility of change feel authentic?
- Do your expectations make you feel hopeful and excited? Or do they create apprehension, dread, or disappointment?
- If the latter, consider how you would you like to change your expectations and why it is important to do so even if it feels uncomfortable.

Once you are able to shift your expectations and see your power in making choices, your actions will follow suit. This allows you to break out of patterns you felt forced to accept.

STAY TRUE TO YOURSELF

As you take steps to deepen your connection with others, it is imperative that you begin to create a routine or ritual around honoring your needs and the process of greater self-understanding. These steps will bring about a significant change in your quality of life, but they can take time. Be patient with the seeds you are planting. Here is a list I often go through with clients to assess how they can exchange unsatisfying activities for ones that are more fulfilling.

- Keep a journal for your thoughts, dreams, and experiences. Try to write in it daily, even if it's just a few lines.
- Keep a clean home. Get rid of things that do not serve you or that you don't really need. Clearing your physical space of clutter will support you in clearing out the internal clutter.
- Create a routine of planning for the week ahead, making time for your social, emotional, and physical needs. Make sure there is at least one activity you enjoy.
- Clean out your social media and unfollow any account that does not align with your values or makes you feel worse about yourself.
- Create a list of books you would like to read so you never become stuck wondering what to read next, or join a book club.

YOUR DREAMS AND GOALS

You may have a list in your mind or may be afraid to have such a list exist even loosely. But, again, expectations result in action and manifestation. Allow yourself to think big here and journal about what dreams you have for your life and specific goals you would like to achieve. Consider the motivation behind these dreams and whether they are yours or someone else's. Continue to reassess and change as needed.

IF YOU ARE STILL HURTING

After reading this book, you may feel that you need further support in understanding and healing your loneliness. I have included a list of studies, books, and other forms of support in the Resources section. Making the decision to begin therapy is also a profound step toward healing, and having a therapist's support and guidance will help you remain accountable in applying the tools outlined in this book.

Additionally, group therapy is a powerful way to address your loneliness among peers who are also struggling but seeking change. The journey toward healing requires surrendering and at least a degree of faith that you deserve something better than your present state. Committing yourself to continuing your process of growth and self-acceptance will open you up to more forms of love. This also requires you to trust in others, and, most important, yourself. Technically, the solution to loneliness is connection, yet it involves so much more. You must look inward, at the feelings and beliefs you hold about yourself and the world around you, and strive toward peace and acceptance within yourself, allowing you to achieve the deep and authentic connections you are searching for.

AFFIRMATIONS

All things will pass, and so shall this.

I am cultivating meaningful connections.

I face my fears with compassion and courage.

I am intentional about building a life I love.

I trust the process.

RESOURCES

WEBSITES

"How to be Alone": www.youtube.com /watch?v=k7X7sZzSXYs

"The Loneliness Project": www.youtube.com /watch?v=IYc85A8f2CM

No Isolation: www.noisolation.com/global

Shani Silver: www.shanisilver.com

"Women Are Happier without Children or a Spouse, Says Happiness Expert": www.theguardian.com/lifeandstyle/2019 /may/25/women-happier-without -children-or-a-spouse-happiness-expert

BOOKS

The Art of Loving by Erich Fromm

The Highly Sensitive Person in Love: Understanding and Managing Relationships When the World Overwhelms You by Elaine N. Aron, PhD

How to Be an Adult in Relationships: The Five Keys to Mindful Loving by David Richo

Mindful Relationship Habits: 25 Practices for Couples to Enhance Intimacy, Nurture Closeness, and Grow a Deeper Connection by S. J. Scott and Barrie Davenport

Perfect Love, Imperfect Relationships: Healing the Wound of the Heart by John Welwood

Why Him? Why Her? Finding Real Love by Understanding Your Personality Type by Helen Fisher

The Wisdom of a Broken Heart: An Uncommon Guide to Healing, Insight, and Love by Susan Piver

REFERENCES

CHAPTER 1

Ballard, Jamie. "Millennials Are the Loneliest Generation." YouGov. July 14, 2009. https://today.yougov.com/topics /lifestyle/articles-reports/2019/07/30 /loneliness-friendship-new-friends-poll-survey.

Cacioppo, John T. *Loneliness: Human Nature and the Need for Social Connection* (Scranton: W. W. Norton & Company, 2009).

Cacioppo, Stephanie et al. "Loneliness: Clinical Import and Interventions." *Perspectives on Psychological Science* 10, no. 2 (March 1, 2015): 238–49. https://doi .org/10.1177/1745691615570616.

"How Loneliness Affects Us." Happify. Accessed October 3, 2019. https://www.happify.com/hd /how-loneliness-affects-us/

Lou, Michelle, and Brandon Griggs. "Acceptance Rates at Top Colleges Are Dropping, Raising Pressure on High School Students." CNN. April 4, 2019. https://edition.cnn.com/2019/04/03/us /ivy-league-college-admissions-trnd/index.html.

Primack, Brian A. et al. "Positive and Negative Experiences on Social Media and Perceived Social Isolation." *American Journal of Health Promotion* 33, no. 6 (July 1, 2019): 859–68. https://doi.org/10.1177/0890117118824196.

"UCLA Loneliness Scale." Self Report Measures for Love and Compassion Research: *Loneliness and Interpersonal Problems*, Fetzer Institute, accessed October 3, 2019. https://fetzer .org/sites/default/files/images/stories/pdf /selfmeasures/Self_Measures_for_Loneliness _and_Interpersonal_Problems_UCLA _LONELINESS.pdf.

CHAPTER 2

Chapman, A. L. "Dialectical Behavior Therapy: Current Indications and Unique Elements." *Psychiatry* (Edgemont) 3, no. 9 (September 2006): 62–68. https://www.ncbi.nlm.nih.gov/pubmed/20975829.

Feller, Samantha. "A Guided Meditation for Self-Love." Yoga International. Accessed October 3, 2019. https://yogainternational.com/article/view/guided-meditation-for-self-love.

Neff, Kristin. "Definition of Self-Compassion." Self-Compassion. Accessed October 3, 2019. https://self-compassion.org/the-three-elements-of-self-compassion-2/.

Pakdaman, Shahla et al. "The Role of Attachment Styles and Resilience on Loneliness." *International Journal of Medical Research and Health Sciences* 5, no. 9 (2016): 268–74. https://www.ijmrhs.com/medical-research/the-role-of-attachment-styles-and-resilience-on-loneliness.pdf.

Panos, Patrick T. et al. "Meta-Analysis and Systematic Review Assessing the Efficacy of Dialectical Behavior Therapy (DBT). *Research on Social Work Practice* 24, no. 2 (March 2014): 213–23. https://doi.org/10.1177/1049731513503047.

Piver, Susan. *The Wisdom of a Broken Heart: An Uncommon Guide to Healing, Insight, and Love* (New York: Atria Books, 2009).

Rosenberg, Ross. "Is Your Life Plagued by Loneliness? Tips to Overcome It." *HuffPost*. Updated December 7, 2017. https://www .huffpost.com/entry/loneliness_b_4648417.

Valentine, Sarah E. et al. "The Use of Dialectical Behavior Therapy Skills Training as Stand-Alone Treatment: A Systematic Review of the Treatment Outcome Literature." *Journal of Clinical Psychology* 71, no. 1 (January 2015): 1–20. https://doi.org/10.1002/jclp.22114.

CHAPTER 3

Orth, Ulrich, Kali H. Trzesniewski, and Richard W. Robins. "Self-Esteem Development from Young Adulthood to Old Age: A Cohort-Sequential Longitudinal Study." *Journal of Personality and Social Psychology* 98, no. 4 (April 2010): 645–58. https://doi.org/10.1037/a0018769.

CHAPTER 4

Chopra, Deepak. "Are You Secretly Lonely?" Oprah.com. March 26, 2014. http://www.oprah.com/inspiration /deepak-chopra-the-signs-of-loneliness /all#ixzz5r7fUNeCO.

Maitland, Sara. *How to Be Alone* (New York: Picador, 2014).

Neyfakh, Leon. "The Power of Lonely." *Boston Globe*. March 6, 2011. http://archive.boston.com /bostonglobe/ideas/articles/2011/03/06 /the_power_of_lonely/.

Turkle, Sherry. "Connected, but Alone?" TED Talk. February 2012. Video, 19:33. https://www.ted.com/talks/sherry _turkle_alone_together#t-3926.

CHAPTER 5

McKay, Matthew, and Patrick Fanning. *Self-Esteem* (New York: MJF Books, 1992).

Romanoff, Zan. "Two Writers on the Joys of Being Single, But Also Sometimes Dating, in Your 30s." *Healthyish*. June 12, 2019. https://www.bonappetit.com/story /dating-thirties.

Winfrey, Oprah. "The Power of No, Part 1: Oprah Winfrey." Interview by Cheryl Strayed. *Dear Sugars*, July 15, 2017. Audio, 35:03. https://www.wbur.org/dearsugar/2017/07/15 /dear-sugars-oprah.

CHAPTER 6

Bayes-Fleming, Nicole. "How Solitude Helps Us Heal." *Mindful*. August 18, 2018. https:// www.mindful.org/how-loneliness-helps-us-heal/.

Cuddy, Amy. "Your Body Language May Shape Who You Are." TEDGlobal 2012. June 2012. Video, 20:48. https://www.ted.com/talks /amy_cuddy_your_body_language_shapes _who_you_are?utm_source=tedcomshare&utm _medium=referral&utm_campaign=tedspread.

Mordini, Silvia. "5 Reasons Why Traveling Solo Can Remedy Loneliness." *The Culture-ist*. July 23, 2013. https://www.thecultureist.com /2013/07/23/traveling-solo-to-cope-with -loneliness/.

Rhimes, Shonda. *Year of Yes: How to Dance It Out, Stand in the Sun and Be Your Own Person* (New York: Simon & Schuster, 2015).

Wiseman, Theresa. "Toward a Holistic Conceptualization of Empathy for Nursing Practice." *Advances in Nursing Science* 30, no. 3 (July–September 2007): E61–72. http://doi .org/10.1097/01.ANS.0000286630.00011.e3.

—"A Concept Analysis of Empathy." *Journal of Advanced Nursing* 23, no. 6 (June 1996): 1162–67. https://doi.org/10.1046/j.1365-2648.1996.12213.x.

CHAPTER 7

"Green Spaces Deliver Lasting Mental Health Benefits." University of Exeter. January 7, 2014. https://www.exeter.ac.uk/news/featurednews /title_349054_en.html.

Jordan, Rob. "Stanford Researchers Find Mental Health Prescription: Nature." *Stanford News*. June 30, 2015. https://news.stanford .edu/2015/06/30/hiking-mental-health-063015/.

Kornfield, Jack. "Walking Meditation." JackKornfield.com. Accessed October 3, 2019. https://jackkornfield.com/walking-meditation-2/.

INDEX

ACKNOWLEDGMENTS

Writing this book has been one of the richest experiences of my life. It has refreshed my eyes to the exquisite beauty of human connection and love. An encounter with another, no matter how small, has the potential to leave an indelible mark on the course of a life.

Merci beaucoup, Paris, for welcoming me into your hot summer arms and inspiring the words of this book. To my new and old Parisian friends, Jonathan, Pamela from Canada, Emilie, Sharon, Mark, Hubert-Jean, Mariam, Lily, and Sophie; thank you for engaging this American and sharing a piece of yourselves and your story with me. And to Henri-Brieuc, *tu es un cadeau à mon coeur.*

I am indebted to the following women for their support in the writing of this book: Roya Bahrami, Laura Fraser, Rochelle Greenhagen, Lauren Korshak, Ana Mazdyasni, and my editor, Emily Angell. Thank you to my fellow masterminds and mentors, Kristina Blachere, Olga Rocklin, Lea Seigen Shinraku, Jodie Stein, Jessica Engle, Adam Bloom, Marie Forleo, Linda Shanti McCabe, Christine Pappas, and Nova Goldberg for the encouragement to make my personal and professional dreams a reality. My Evolve Wellness team: Erika Bent, Sarah

Calloway, Anna Clark, Kari Floberg, Cora Keene, Natalie Makardish, and Jennifer Simmons; you are all a great blessing to me and the clients you support in living the lives they deserve.

In memory of the beautiful souls that recently left this world too soon, Jonathan McCabe and Emma Kennedy.

To my clients, thank you for being my greatest teachers of vulnerability, strength, and the perseverance of the human spirit. Mam'noon Maman Bazorg and the rest of my big, beautiful family in Iran. You are what defines family to me.

To my soul sisters Sara Aslan, Kathryn Clark-Hilliard, Alma Dumitru, Sarah Forsberg, Anny Ha, Catherine Mevs, Jenny Ng, and Mitra Pai; thank you for always being my cheerleaders in this game of life.

My angels, Reza Baalbaki, Maysan Bahrami, and Zahra Baalbaki; thank you for the joy you add to each and every day.

Thank you, Mom, for instilling in me the belief that I am worthy, loved, and accepted unconditionally.

Dad, *merci* for teaching me to honor myself and every living thing with respect and reverence. *Je vous aime tous.*

ABOUT THE AUTHOR

 Shrein H. Bahrami is a marriage and family therapist in San Francisco. She is the founder of Evolve Wellness, a group practice of clinicians specializing in the treatment of relationships, anxiety, and eating disorders. Shrein is the author of *Stop Bingeing, Start Living: Proven Therapeutic Strategies for Breaking the Binge Eating Cycle* and has contributed to articles featured in *NBC News*, the *Guardian*, *Bustle*, *Reader's Digest*, and the *Mighty*.

CPSIA information can be obtained
at www.ICGtesting.com
Printed in the USA
BVHW091438261119
564831BV00018B/348/P